ERIC ROHMER
CLAUDE CHABROL

HITCHCOCK

THE FIRST
FORTY-FOUR FILMS

TRANSLATED BY STANLEY HOCHMAN

FREDERICK UNGAR PUBLISHING CO.

New York

Translator's dedication:
To my wife—

S.H.

Translated from the French *Hitchcock*
by arrangement with S.A. Editions Universitaires / Jean-Pierre Delarge Editeur

Copyright © 1979 by Frederick Ungar Publishing Co., Inc.
Printed in the United States of America
Designed by Jacqueline Schuman
Second Printing, 1980

Library of Congress Cataloging in Publication Data

Rohmer, Eric, 1920–
  Hitchcock, the first forty-four films.

  Filmography: p.
  Includes index.
  1. Hitchcock, Alfred Joseph, 1899–   I. Chabrol,
Claude, 1930–   joint author.   II. Title.
PN1998.A3H5513   1979   791.43′0233′0924   78-20538
ISBN 0-8044-2743-7
ISBN 0-8044-6749-8 pbk.

CONTENTS

1

THE ENGLISH PERIOD

2

THE AMERICAN PERIOD (1): WITH SELZNICK   *57*

3

_____

THE AMERICAN PERIOD (2):
ROPE TO *THE MAN WHO KNEW TOO MUCH*
(1948–1956)

4

_____

CONCLUSION: *THE WRONG MAN* (1957)　145

TRANSLATOR'S NOTE

Another book on Hitchcock? No, not another book, but finally *the* book on Hitchcock, the almost legendary work that focused critical attention on a director too many film critics tended to dismiss as a "mere entertainer."

In 1957, two brilliant contributors to France's influential *Cahiers du Cinéma,* who were themselves soon to become film directors of international status, published the first book-length study of Alfred Hitchcock. Fifteen years later there were nine others, but in his introduction to *Focus on Hitchcock* (1972), an anthology of critical articles, Albert J. LaValley pointed out that in spite of its still controversial nature "the Rohmer-Chabrol thesis had the effect of launching a major debate, which has been conducted ever since under the shadow of its terms."

Most critics have generously acknowledged the importance of this youthful work even when, like Robin Wood, they ultimately rejected aspects of the rigorously Catholic analyses. "Eric Rohmer and Claude Chabrol deserve our gratitude for their pioneer work," Wood wrote in 1966. "(T)heir book on Hitchcock constitutes a very serious attempt to account for the resonances his films can evoke in the mind. One admires its many brilliant perceptions and the authors' interest in the moral qualities of Hitchcock's films."

For over twenty years the vagaries of publishing economics kept this influential study from being available to American film buffs and scholars. Publishers concerned with "the bottom line" shied away from a Hitchcock book that included analyses—however insightful and influential—of only the auteur's first forty-four films. They seemed unconvinced by the argument that what was past was prelude and that all that came afterward could only be understood in the light of what had already been accomplished. As interest in film history mushroomed, however, *zamizdat* translations circulated from hand to hand.

The Rohmer/Chabrol *Hitchcock,* considered by many the "key Hitchcock critique,"* compares in importance with D. H. Lawrence's brilliant *Studies in Classic American Literature,* which rescued American classics by Poe, Hawthorne, Melville, and Cooper from their consignment to the realm of "children's books. Just childishness, on our part." Like that seminal study by the English creative and critical genius, this seminal study by two French creative and critical geniuses is sometimes impatient with details. However, none of the minor discrepancies due to slips of memory or the fact that some of the films may have been viewed in French release versions affect the basic and fascinating insights offered into the work of one of our major film auteurs. My thanks to Maurice Yacowar for helping to restore the long-lost exclamation mark to *Murder!*

Stanley Hochman

*Choice, November 1977

FOREWORD

It may seem foolhardy to undertake a detailed analysis of Alfred
Hitchcock's first forty-four films in a book of this size. Nevertheless, after rejecting two other approaches that initially seemed
more promising, this is exactly what we proposed to do.

Our first idea was to follow a logical rather than a chronological
order and to isolate both the themes ordinarily found in our
director and the general characteristics of his style. But it is always
a mistake to separate content from the means of its expression,
and in the case of the man who made *Rope,* the problems of form
and substance are especially closely connected. The idea of the
"exchange," which we find everywhere in his work, may be given
either a moral expression (the transfer of guilt), a psychological
expression (suspicion), a dramatic expression (blackmail—or even
pure "suspense"), or a concrete expression (a to-and-fro movement). Isolating these different motifs artificially would have
necessitated a perpetual and tiresome backtracking from film to
film.

Our second idea had been to make a detailed study of only
certain important or significant films at the expense of the others.
But how were we to choose? Which are the good and which the
bad vintages? Even the technical experiments are less technical
than they seem, and the commercial works less commercial.
Should the English period be sacrificed? Though we consider these

apprentice years to be somewhat less significant than other critics
find them, a number of Hitchcock's early films are not unworthy of
those that were to follow, and it seemed a good idea to let the
reader profit from our recent opportunity to see them at the
cinémathèque.

We therefore decided to follow a strict chronological approach.
In this way we have had the pleasure of watching the slow genesis
of a body of work that is varied enough to enable us to avoid being
repetitious and unified enough to allow a homogeneity of approach. Every Hitchcock film is based on a sort of "formal
postulate," which most often only needs to be pointed out. This
postulate is particularly evident in the more recent* works—the
most rigorously constructed—and therefore, beginning with *Rope*
(1948), we have used a subtitle to indicate the dominant theme of
our commentary.

There is no need for further preamble. Our technique is based
on familiarization: it is by familiarizing oneself with his work that
one learns to appreciate and love Hitchcock; the important thing is
to observe an order, a gradation, as in piano exercises. We have
therefore been content to work toward the depths slowly, hoping
that our final insights will inevitably illuminate earlier commentary
retrospectively, just as Hitchcock's films throw mutual and
instructive light on one another.

*Translator's note: This was written in 1957.

Let's say I'm like a painter who paints flowers. What interests me is the way in which things are treated. But on the other hand, if I were a painter, I would say: "I can only paint something that contains a message."

Alfred Hitchcock

Full fathom five they father lies;
Of his bones are coral made;
Those are pearls that were his eyes;
Nothing of him that doth fade
But doth suffer a sea-change
Into something *rich and strange*.

The Tempest, Act 1, Scene 2

HITCHCOCK

THE ENGLISH PERIOD

Alfred Joseph Hitchcock was born in London on August 13, 1899. His father, a native of Essex, was a poultry merchant and a Catholic. Alfred was brought up rather strictly: his father was a strong believer in discipline and knew how to impose unusual and impressive punishments. For example, one day young Alfred decided on a brief escapade and indulged in his favorite pastime—bus rides from one end of the city to the other. Papa Hitchcock, who was a friend of the local police commissioner, staged a dramatic scene that ended with his prodigal son spending the night in jail. If Alfred Hitchcock is to be believed, his fear of policemen stems from this incident alone. But is he really afraid of policemen?

Young Alfred studied under the Jesuits at Saint Ignatius College. He was a good if not particularly outstanding student, except perhaps in geography. In his room, Alfred had an enormous map of the world on which he would stick small flags to mark the movement of British ships. He was mathematically inclined and could draw quite well. Naturally enough, he wanted to be an engineer. It was to this endeavor that he initally turned on leaving the Jesuit Fathers—who, he says, had taught him to see things from a "practical" point of view.

His engineering studies were short-lived. Art attracted him—so much so that he took night-school classes in it before joining an advertising agency, where he prepared dummies of posters for fifteen shillings a week. He wasn't there long before he decided that he preferred the W.T. Henley Telegraph Company. In this very respectable firm he acquired the undesirable reputation of a prankster by savagely caricaturing the higher-ups and administrators.

But Alfred Joseph Hitchcock was in love with the movies. He haunted Wardour Street in hopes of ferreting out a job in film-making. He was lucky. In 1920, with the help of an actor who sometimes worked at Henley's, he was able to get a job as a title designer. He soon became head of the Titling Section of a newly organized American firm. The Famous Players–Lasky had big plans: it had just established the Islington studios to launch a series of "international" productions, with English and American stars working under Hollywood directors.

And thus it was that for two years Hitchcock wrote and designed titles for such films as Hugh Ford's *The Great Day* and *Call of Youth;* Donald Crisp's *Princess of New York* and *Tell Your Children;* George Fitzmaurice's *Three Live Ghosts* (starring Edmond Goulding), etc. Hitchcock worked hard, well, and quickly. He was appreciated. The director of a film, *Always Tell Your Wife* (1922), fell sick during shooting. Hitchcock, who was always circling around the set, noticed that the lead actor, Seymour Hicks, seemed upset because he had to undertake the direction of the movie and he was short on ideas. The "fat young man" enthusiastically came to his aid and helped him complete the film.

The First Gainsborough Films (1923–1927)

Having once tried his hand at directing, Hitchcock understood that this was where his vocation lay. Unable to wait any longer, he joined with actress Clare Greet and, at twenty-three, produced and directed his first film—*Number Thirteen* (1922), which dealt with London's lower classes.

Lack of capital kept the film from ever being completed, but the time he spent on it was by no means wasted. When Famous Players–Lasky stopped production at Islington, Michael Balcon, who took over the studio, appointed Hitchcock assistant director for *Woman to Woman* (1922), which was being filmed by Graham Cutts. Alfred was so active that he also did the scenario, which was based on a play by Michael Morton.

Michael Balcon continued to rely on him, giving him the triple role of assistant director, artistic director, and editor of four other Graham Cutts films: *The Prude's Fall* (1923), *The White Shadow* (1923), *The Passionate Adventure* (1924), and *The Blackguard* (1925).

This last film was shot in Germany at the UFA studios in Neubabelsberg. The system of Anglo-German coproduction seemed so advantageous to Balcon that he decided to associate himself with the Emelka Company and make two more films, this time in Munich. He managed to have Hitchcock appointed director for these films: *The Pleasure Garden* (1925) and *The Mountain Eagle* (1926).

It's difficult to judge these two works since we haven't seen them, and Hitchcock, who doesn't care for them, would just as soon forget about them. According to contemporary reviews, on which it is best not to rely too strongly, *The Pleasure Garden* was a success and *The Mountain Eagle* a semi-failure. Nevertheless, both were cited for their "brilliant direction."

The subjects of these films are—to say the least—strange:

The Pleasure Garden relates the misadventures of a chorus girl who gets a part for her friend, a woman who soon lets success go to her head and breaks with her fiancé, who has gone to the Tropics. The heroine marries a friend of this fiancé, and her husband also takes off for the Tropics. Finally, she too goes to the Tropics, where she is disagreeably surprised to find her husband living a dissolute and adulterous life. Her husband's mistress is an apparent suicide, and the husband himself dies in an earthquake after having beaten up his wife. The heroine returns to England on the arm of the former fiancé of her former protegée.

The Mountain Eagle is stranger still. In a small Kentucky town a young schoolteacher is harassed first by the hostility and then by the amorous attentions of the owner of a local emporium. When she rejects these attentions, he accuses her of trying to seduce his son and incites the entire town against her. The teacher flees to the mountains, where she meets up with a handsome hermit named Fear O'God. He takes her under his wing, and the two of them return to the town, where he intends to marry her under the very nose of the storekeeper. The latter, furious, profits from the fact that his son has run away to accuse Fear O'God of having murdered him. The unfortunate hermit is tried, found guilty, and imprisoned. A year later he escapes and takes refuge in the mountains with his wife and child. After a variety of complications, the storekeeper's son returns to the paternal hearth and all ends well.

No doubt these plots—furnished by Eliot Stannard, who was for some time to be Hitchcock's official scenario writer—are open to endless criticism. However, there is no reason to doubt that the films were extremely interesting. In any case, they established their director's reputation.

As good as they may have been, these initial efforts have no value in the eyes of Hitchcock, who dates the beginning of his career from *The Lodger* (1926), his first big success and—is it only a coincidence?—his first "suspense" film.

The Lodger was adapted by Eliot Stannard and Hitchcock himself from a well-known and widely praised novel by Mrs. Belloc-Lowndes.[1] This was Hitch's first collaboration on a scenario, a fact from which we can draw two conclusions: first, that Balcon already had a great deal of confidence in him; second, that the subject especially interested him and, to his way of thinking, would allow him to make a big splash. He was right. The film was very favorably received by both the critics and the public, and in a cinematic milieu that was already hardening, the name Hitchcock became known overnight.

[1]There were to be several film versions of this book: in 1933 by Maurice Elvey (once more with Ivor Novello), in 1944 by John Brahm (with Laird Cregar), and in 1954 by Hugo Fregonese (*The Man in the Attic*, with Jack Palance).

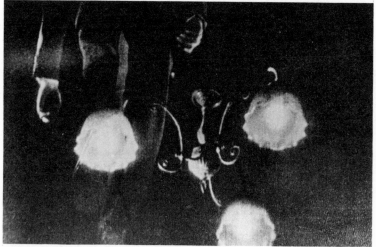

"The subjects of these films are—to say the least—strange." A dead native girl appears to the delirious protagonist of *The Pleasure Garden* (1925) and orders the death of his wife. (PHOTO FROM BRITISH NATIONAL FILM ARCHIVE)

Ivor Novello in the title role of *The Lodger* (1926) paces a glass floor that allows us to see what his worried landlady hears in this silent version of Mrs. Belloc-Lowndes's novel. (PHOTO FROM BRITISH NATIONAL FILM ARCHIVE)

The fact is that the greater part of what was to become known as the famous "Hitchcock touch" is already to be found in this well-constructed variation on the theme of Jack the Ripper.

The scenario is as follows. London is terrorized by a homicidal maniac, "The Avenger." A young man comes to a family boarding house, where his strange behavior soon arouses the suspicions of his landlady—especially as he begins courting her daughter, the fiancée of a detective. Denounced to the police and arrested, the young man flees—handcuffed—and is chased by a mob intent on lynching him. At the last minute, the true guilty party is discovered. The stranger will eventually marry his landlady's daughter.

Certain themes or details that are frequently to be repeated in later works are already present in this film: the innocent man against whom appearances unite and whose behavior inevitably suggests guilt; handcuffs, symbol of lost liberty; objects (in this case a poker) on which suspicion confers an erroneously menacing role. We also note an obsession with Christian iconography: the hero, attached to a railing by his handcuffs and hooted by the crowd, irresistibly suggests the image of Christ on the cross.

The Lodger demonstrates Hitchcock's virtuosity and remarkable visual sense. The opening of the film is dazzling: a close-up of a man's hand on a stairway banister; a pan shot discloses the stairwell in which light and shadow are ominously apportioned. The man goes into the night. Shot of a newspaper announcing a new crime.

Effects of this kind abound throughout the film, as does a certain photographic preciosity—like that amazing shot showing the body of a woman whose blond hair (the killer prefers blonds) is lit from below and pierces the darkness. Another example is the worm's-eye view which, thanks to a glass floor, reveals the stranger pacing back and forth in his room.

This virtuosity is not completely free of cynicism. It already reveals that spirit of mystification which Hitchcock was not to bring under control until much later, and which mars some of his English films. But there are, of course, excuses for it. The point was to make a big splash and show that you were somebody with

A disgraced young student (Ivor Novello) has a short-lived relationship with an actress (Isabel Jeans) whom he marries in *Downhill* (1927), based on a Novello play. (PHOTO FROM BRITISH NATIONAL FILM ARCHIVE)

whom the industry would henceforth have to reckon. From this tactical point of view, Hitch was completely successful, and we may well consider this showy side of *The Lodger* as an indication of his faultless sense of publicity and commercial considerations. This same spirit will be evident, in a more disagreeable form, in *Sabotage* (1936), when Hitchcock wanted to leave no doubt about his "international" status and to consolidate his standing in view of an eventual departure for Hollywood. For all this, *The Lodger* is nonetheless a film that throws a great deal of light on the tendencies of our cineast. In the person of its leading man, Ivor Novello, it furnishes the perfect example of a certain type of Hitchcockian actor: handsome, disturbing, projecting a strange and melancholy gentleness with romantic overtones. It should be noted that the acting is very good (Hitchcock very quickly obtained perfection on this point), particularly on the part of Malcolm Keen (the detective), whom Hitch was to use again in *The Manxman* (1929), and Marie Ault (the landlady).

As we have said, the film's success was considerable. The Hitchcock-Novello association seemed so advantageous to the producers that the following year Gainsborough confided to Hitchcock the film adaptation of *Downhill* (1927), a play by Novello, in which the popular actor obviously starred. Contemporary critics were greatly disappointed by the film; however, their judgment now strikes us as severe and unjust. Obviously, these critics had formed a false idea of Hitchcock (nor was this to be the last time that would happen!) and they held the director responsible for not confirming that idea. However, those of us who see *Downhill* today find a number of fine qualities in it, and it is possible to prefer it to *The Lodger*.

True, the story is a mediocre one: a young student, the son of a respectable family, is accused of a theft committed by a roommate whom for reasons of honor he does not denounce. He is expelled from school and disowned by his father. He has a short-lived relationship with an actress and becomes a ballroom dancer in Paris, where the older women are unable to keep their eyes off him. Then he finds himself in the slums of Marseilles. In a state of physical and moral delirium, he stows away on a ship which he thinks is heading South but which instead takes him back to England, where his parents welcome him like the prodigal son.

To begin with, let us note that this plot—whatever its value—has nothing of the thriller or suspense story about it. After the success of *The Lodger,* it would have been easy for Hitchcock to become a specialist in that genre. He preferred instead to try his hand at something else, but his previous success eventually led him to entrench himself in the thriller. And even so, he always interpreted the genre very freely.

But let us return to *Downhill.* He found in it only three places for touching up scenes by showing his gifts as a creator of atmosphere, as a satirist, and as a camera virtuoso.

The school at the beginning is depicted with a rare truthfulness: the sequence abounds in amusing and critical observations. The sketches of the teachers, the students, and the parents are clearly done. But the film especially reveals Hitchcock as a remarkable painter of depravity. In this regard, the scene in the Paris nightclub offers a gallery of portraits that are terrifying in their accuracy and cruelty: the faces of the avid-eyed, slack-cheeked older women almost seem to justify the charge of misogyny so often brought against Hitchcock. These are certainly the "monstrous females" who are systematically done in by Uncle Charlie in *Shadow of a Doubt* (1943). However, as we shall see, this misogyny is only seeming and stems from an exalted conception of women.

It should also be noted that in *Downhill* we have the first instance of that notion of "itinerary," which is often to be found in future blms.[1]

The hero's fall follows a specific direction: from North to South. He literally descends. This idea is clearly expressed by the mise-en-scène in the subjective Marseilles delirium sequence, which consists of descending stairways and gangways. The virtuosity of the technique employed makes the sequence an illustration of a psychological and moral idea, an excellent example of the interdependence of form and substance. One can understand what Hitchcock means when he says that he is less interested in the subject treated than in the way it is treated; or when he explains that he conceives a film as "a form: lines moving in a given direction." We will often have occasion to return to this point. Let us simply note that in *Downhill* the school is treated in a horizontal forward track, the nightclub in a series of pans expressing stagnation, and the port of Marseilles in a vertical track from top to bottom.

Thus, though at first glance the direction of *Downhill* may

[1]For example, in *Rich and Strange, The Thirty-Nine Steps, Young and Innocent, The Lady Vanishes, Saboteur, Foreign Correspondent, Spellbound,* and *The Man Who Knew Too Much.*

appear less brilliant than that of *The Lodger,* it is no less effective.
It is certainly more "thought out," and it marks a step forward.
The film's lack of success interrupted these formal experiments for
some time.

An additional consequence of its failure was that Gainsborough
forced on Hitchcock the adaptation of *Easy Virtue* (1927), a play
by Noel Coward. This time the task imposed was to provide no
compensating advantages. Nothing in this story of a divorcée
unable to rebuild her life was of interest to Hitch. He relied
completely on his craftsmanship and managed to get the job done
creditably thanks to a careful though somewhat lusterless direction, plus a perfect handling of the leading lady, Isabel Jeans. The
film cruelly underlined the artificiality and the shallowness of
Coward's play. For Hitchcock it was an elegant way of thumbing
his nose at Gainsborough and reclaiming his freedom.

End of the Silents—Beginning of the Talkies— British International (1927–1932)

He had managed very well. At twenty-seven he was officially
considered the great hope of English cinema. The films shot for
Michael Balcon included one triumph (*The Lodger*) and five works
that had been variously received, but considered "well directed."
Job offers came from all the British studios. He chose British
International, and John Maxwell as producer. For Maxwell he
made four silent films and six talkies. The best was cheek and jowl
with the worst, but on four occasions the best achieved perfection.
If we had to choose the "golden years" of the English period, we
would go against current opinion and designate those years of his
collaboration with British International rather than those of the
Gaumont–British period (1934–1937) that followed.

This fascinating era began under remarkable auspices. John
Maxwell gave a free hand to Hitchcock, who was simultaneously
the scenario writer, the dialogue writer, and the director of *The
Ring* (1927), which along with *The Manxman* (1929) was his best
silent film.

The plot of *The Ring* is very similar to that of other sports-related films of which audiences at the time were so fond. It has every appearance of a classic and commonplace love triangle. Jack Sander, a midway boxer, is engaged to the ticketseller of the attraction, Nelly, whose flashing eyes bring the rubbernecks in. One of these—Bob Corby, an Australian champion—knocks out Sander and profits from his victory to make love to Nelly. In order to keep her close at hand, he makes Sander his trainer. It is Sander, however, who marries Nelly, and Corby arranges some minor matches for him. But on the evening of one fight, Nelly leaves Sander to join Corby. The two men meet in the ring; Sander is victorious and wins back his wife, but there is a certain ambiguity about the ending.

The plot is obviously very commonplace, but Hitchcock has never feared commonplace plots. Like most of his great successes, *The Ring* has appearances against it. At first glance all it has going for it is the virtuosity of its technique, which is extraordinary for the time and a considerable advance over that in his previous films. There is a masterful use of ellipsis, but this technique was current. What was not current was the sense of the camera's movement and its integration in the montage. What was not current was the way the scenes were thought out, in dramatic and dynamic terms, as parts of a whole and not as a succession of plastic shots. All in all it was a conception of cinema diametrically opposed to that of E. A. Dupont in *Variety*. From this point of view, as André Bazin has noted, *The Ring* makes us think of Renoir.

But even the scenario should not be too quickly dismissed. It permits Hitchcock a very subtle treatment of a theme that is dear to him: adultery. Beneath the surface of popular melodrama, the work is rich in original observations and striking symbols. The title can be understood in several senses: "the ring" is a bracelet that Bob Corby gives the young woman and which all during the film will symbolize adultery. Many effects underscore Hitchcock's intention: depending on the state of her relations with her husband and her lover, Nelly either hides this bracelet or flaunts it, sometimes ashamed, sometimes cruelly triumphant. But a "ring" is also a wedding band, and at one point in the film Hitchcock, who never hesitates to follow through on his symbols, shows Sander taking the bracelet and slipping it onto Nelly's finger as a wedding ring. In an especially fine touch, the bracelet is a representation of a coiled serpent; for the Catholic Hitchcock, adultery is identified with Eve's original sin.

The dazzling ideas sown through this film could be endlessly enumerated. When the husband rips his wife's dress, she covers her breast with a photograph of her lover; when Sander comes home after a bout and organizes a party, champagne flows into glasses, Sander notices his wife's absence and understands that she is with her lover: a close-up of a glass of champagne gone flat.

The carnival with which the film opens is treated at length. Like the good creator of atmosphere that he is, Hitchcock takes his time and multiplies the visual "gags." Not a single grotesquerie escapes him—neither the stupefied aspect of the people milling about the fairground like sleepwalkers nor the obscenity of the swings. He concludes the sequence with two shots of open-mouthed people and a carnival Aunt Sally.

It was with *The Ring* that Hitchcock found "his" chief cameraman, Jack Cox, who was to shoot all his films until 1933. Hitchcock's style is based on precision. The least falling off between the conception and the realization can be fatal. Hitchcock therefore always tried to form an ideal "team," which he attempted to keep together from film to film. From this point of view his work can easily be divided into three periods, each of which corresponds to the perfection of a style. Jack Cox was to be replaced by Bernard Knowles during the Gaumont–British period. During the American period Hitchcock was to take nine years to find his ideal man (though one may note a slight preference for Joseph Valentine). Now [1957] this period has "its" cameraman, Robert Burks, with whom he has worked since *Strangers on a Train*. The quality of Jack Cox's work in the *The Ring* is beyond question. It is characterized by the precision of the frames, by their simplicity, and by the harmony between the grays and whites that was dear to Hitchcock during this period.

It is clear that *The Ring* does more than simply mark the

A widowed farmer (Jameson Thomas, extreme left) watches as his hostess' maid explains that she hadn't known that the fire would melt the ices in a scene from *The Farmer's Wife* (1928). (PHOTO FROM BRITISH NATIONAL FILM ARCHIVE)

transition from one company to another. It is a veritable turning point: the young hope becomes the accomplished auteur whose youth does not preclude mastery. He is famous in Great Britain, and the proof of his fame is that company publications unhesitatingly say: "publicity factor—Hitchcock's name." As we will see, however, his talent has not yet reached its maturity—far from it. Though technique no longer has any secrets from him, he is still incapable of creating a true work. He is still searching.

This is why he chose, after *The Ring*, to do a sort of rustic comedy by Eden Philpotts, *The Farmer's Wife* (1928). He did the adaptation himself. The result was undeniably inferior to *The Ring*, not because the film is bad—within its genre it is a success—but because with it Hitchcock strayed from his true path.

The Farmer's Wife is the story of a farmer, no longer in his first youth, who, after five years of widowhood, decides to remarry. With his housekeeper, Araminta, he works up a list of possible spouses and immediately begins on a round of visits. In his film version, Hitchcock slightly modified the play, in which the farmer's vanity is wounded after he is rejected three times in succession. The film's point of view is somewhat different: the farmer does of course experience rejection, but what really discourages him is the women's behavior. Although in his mind he had embellished them with a considerable number of virtues, each one shows herself to be more affected, bigoted, and intolerable than the last. Misogyny? Not in the light of the conclusion: the farmer marries his housekeeper, who has long been secretly in love with him and who is the ideal wife because a wife is, above all, a housewife. The point of view is that of a man who enjoys his domestic comforts, but it is also that of a man in love with femininity. The proof is that the character of Araminta (played by Lillian Hall-Davies, star of *The Ring*) is the only one to be spared.

What probably interested Hitchcock in *The Farmer's Wife* was the setting—the Welsh countryside, of which, with the help of Jack Cox, he achieved some remarkable photographs. The atmosphere of English rural life at the beginning of the century is reconstructed in great detail. On the other hand, the virtuoso sequences appear out of place in a story that would seem to call for a painstaking and somewhat lackluster realism. The film is, of course, made more amusing by them, but it is nevertheless true that Hitchcock's temperament was not suited to this kind of story. He was perfectly aware of this, for he was not to return to the portrayal of atmosphere unless he was inspired by the presence of a moral conflict—as was the case with *The Manxman* (1929).

But before this, Hitchcock was to make a very different film, an American-type comedy based on a scenario by Eliot Stannard: *Champagne* (1928). It's a very funny comedy, to be sure, but disappointing and merely a marking of time for its auteur. Too much in this film is sacrificed to what Orson Welles has called "pathetic tricks," and it is on the whole no more than a collection of superimpositions, distortions, speed-ups, an outpouring of frills and furbelows, of cumbersome feathers, of grotesque jewels. The satire is funny but superficial, yet even in the midst of this forced humor there is suddenly an unexpected harmony, a moment of gravity: the young harebrained millionairess, whose father has convinced her he's been ruined, takes a job in a nightclub and gets her buttocks pinched by her boss; the father admits his lie and the daughter bursts out in a reproach worthy of Corneille. He never gave thought to her dignity; he doesn't know what dignity is, she complains. A flash of seriousness in a film that tries to portray the superficial and is caught in its own trap. *Champagne* is a failure. Of course, for Hitchcock it's bubbling, but a fly wouldn't drown in its depths.

Contemporary critics were not fooled, and their reservations were in direct proportion to their disappointment. The Hitchcock of *Champagne* was not the one they had hoped for. This reaction is not lacking in piquancy when one notes that present-day critics see in Hitchcock and his works only the equivalent of this amiable trifle.

Luckily, *The Manxman* was the complete antithesis of *Champagne:* a very ambitious film that makes absolutely no concessions. The story is as follows: Pete and Philip are childhood friends and have always lived together in a village on the Isle of Man. The former is a fisherman and the latter a lawyer. Pete is in love with Kate, the daughter of an innkeeper; since he is not much good at words, he sends Philip to ask the girl's father for her hand. As it happens, Philip is himself secretly in love with Kate. He says nothing, but he cannot suppress his joy when the innkeeper refuses to marry his daughter to Pete, who, he points out, is penniless. Hearing this objection, the fisherman decides to go off in search of his fortune. He asks Philip to watch over Kate, who has promised to wait for him.

Once more, it should be noted that the point of departure is extremely ordinary. Hitchcock sketches it in rapidly, applying

himself to a careful definition of the characters and the relations
among them. He takes advantage of the opportunity to give an
exact, unpicturesque portrait of life on the island. There is no
pointless virtuosity here—just a simple and precise shooting script
supported by Jack Cox's lovely images.

At this point, the film takes on a more elevated tone. Philip
sincerely tries to distract Kate, who is sincerely awaiting her
fisherman's return. Their relationship evolves imperceptibly toward an unavowed love. The news of Pete's death comes as a
release. Kate and Philip feel freed of their promises and they make
love. Pete, of course, returns, and when he does, Philip and Kate
decide to keep their secret and renounce their love. Kate marries
Pete and gives birth to a child whose father is really Philip. Pete
still suspects nothing. He is deliriously happy. But Kate, who
remains passionately in love with Philip, asks him to go off with
her. Philip refuses because of his friendship for Pete and also
because of his social position: he wants to be named deemster
(judge), and a scandal such as this would ruin his career. In despair
over this hopeless situation, Kate tries to commit suicide. For this
crime under English law, she is judged by Philip, who at this point
feels himself morally constrained to confess his guilt. The two
lovers tell Pete the truth and make him understand that he must
permit them to take the child. They leave the island together
amidst the jeers of the townspeople.

A plot such as this, melodramatic in its premises, can only
achieve the sublime if the film-maker dares to meet the challenge
head-on. For the first time, Hitchcock penetrated a domain that
has since become dear to him—vertigo. The situation in *The
Manxman* is sublime because it is insoluble and rejects all artifice.
It is insoluble because it does not depend upon the evilness of the
characters or the relentlessness of fate. Hitchcock gave himself up
to a minute, complete, and unflinching description of the moral
conflict opposing three people whose behavior is practically
beyond reproach. Their failing is the failing of all human beings.
Ordinary morality is helpless to resolve their problems. Each one
is obliged to assume his own responsibilities and to forge a
personal ethic. In an opening title, Hitchcock draws our attention

The Manxman (1929) gave Hitchcock the opportunity to present a portrait of life on the Isle of Man. Philip (Malcolm Keen) is a member of a lover's triangle with which he cannot cope. (PHOTO FROM BRITISH NATIONAL FILM ARCHIVE)

to the moral significance of this work: "What shall it profit a man if he gain the whole world and lose his own soul?" The very form of the film participates in this noble inspiration. No more extraneous artifice. The direction is deliberately centered on the faces, on their expressions; the vicissitudes of the plot are pushed into the background. This praiseworthy purity is not achieved without some loss. The "Hitchcock touch," the effectiveness of which had already been proven in *The Ring,* is almost completely absent here—though we should cite the following beautiful scene: after having confessed his offenses to the tribunal, Philip removes his judge's wig as though it were a mask and resigns.

Perhaps it is this austerity that is the basis of the incomprehension that greeted *The Manxman.* Yet it is a film that goes straight to its goal. If it brings any name to mind, it is Griffith's. But what the critics expected from Hitchcock was only brio, which they already were interpreting as a sign of his superficiality. (It is obvious that *The Manxman* is not a simple melodrama—that Hitchcock neither conceived nor directed it as a melodrama. On the contrary, he made every effort to extirpate the moral core that fascinated him from its surrounding melodramatic gangue.) This failure of critical vision is serious when it comes to an auteur who is above all a director. It is well to note that Hitchcock, who now talks of his English period with a certain repugnance, does not in any way reject this beautiful film.

Two consecutive semi-failures, even if one of them is unjustly considered so, never do a film-maker's career any good. The reputation of the London "wonder boy" was in danger of being badly damaged. Hitch was perfectly aware of this. His career was at stake, so he decided to renounce his "experiments" and, for the first time—without, however, stooping to "made to order" films—try to come to terms with commercial imperatives. Examining his films, Hitch noted that *The Lodger* had been his greatest commercial and even critical success. He therefore looked around for a good thriller and found it in a play by Charles Bennett. The producers immediately gave him a free hand. Hitchcock's acquired

Alice (Anny Ondra) slips into a costume at the urging of the Artist (Cyril Ritchard), whom she will shortly murder for attempted rape in *Blackmail* (1929). (PHOTO FROM BRITISH NATIONAL FILM ARCHIVE)

mastery and an unexpected event—the birth of sound—enabled *Blackmail* (1929) to surpass all hopes.

Hitchcock's last silent film, it was converted into the first British talkie. *Blackmail* is also the auteur's first example of a "premeditated" film. Among other things, it contains a balanced dosage of commercial elements and creative will, of "concession" and "message." As was always to be the case, the scenario is the "concession," the direction the "message."

Alice, the fiancée of a detective, lets herself be picked up in a restaurant by a painter, who takes her to his studio. He apparently tries to rape her. To defend her virtue, which one would have thought to be less precious to her, she stabs him with a breadknife. An unknown man has seen the young girl with the painter and attempts to blackmail her. But suspicion turns against the black-mailer thanks to the detective, who, persuaded of his fiancée's innocence (despite the proof he has of her escapade), in turn blackmails the scoundrel. Pursued by the police, the blackmailer is trapped on the roof of the British Museum and falls through a skylight to his death. The case is closed. Alice nevertheless confesses her crime to the detective.

Hitchcock likes to point out that he had initially planned a different ending: Alice, wanted for murder, tries to flee with the help of her fiancé. Some other policemen track them down and congratulate the detective on having arrested the murderess. She is imprisoned, and a policeman says to the fiancé: "Going out with your girl tonight?" "No, not tonight," the detective replies. This is certainly the way the play ends. If Hitchcock didn't retain that ending, it was not, as might be thought, for commercial reasons, but on the contrary out of personal preference. The end he substituted is actually very similar to that of some of his later works.

The entire film focuses on the relationships among the charac-ters. Victims and victimizers alternate from sequence to sequence: the victimizer becomes the victim, the victim the victimizer. In the same scene, sometimes in a single shot, the moral positions of the protagonists shift. Take, for example, the short scene between the blackmailer and the detective: the latter is on the right; then, when to save his fiancée the detective in turn suggests an ignoble bargain to the blackmailer, he places himself on the left of the frame. The position of the characters expresses their relationship. This touch is really "pure Hitchcock." The principle was to be refined by the director and reworked a number of times in his American films.

As a matter of fact, the entire film is constructed with this in mind: Hitchcock was less interested in telling a story in linear fashion than in using cinematic means to impose the point of view from which it was to be seen. Thus the first ten minutes of the film do not appear to advance the action: they show the arrest of a criminal and the different phases of police procedure. Their only function is to indicate the punishment the heroine will incur after her crime. It is a threat; it is also—and above all—an indication of the *price* that society demands be paid for crime. The denouement will show us that in refusing to pay the price Alice will have to submit to a *moral* punishment, which Hitchcock is careful to suggest without defining. What he does is make use of a symbol that is perhaps simplistic but nonetheless striking: the painting of a snickering clown. This painting, which the terrified Alice gazes at in the artist's studio immediately after the murder, will be shown in a final image to be staring at the couple as they move off. It doesn't so much represent remorse as it does the crime itself—the crime which at this final moment cannot be washed away. Hitchcock was often to use this type of symbol in the future—in *The Thirty-Nine Steps, The Paradine Case, Under Capricorn, Stage Fright, I Confess,* etc.

Blackmail also prefigures other aspects of films to come: the description of a woman's torments, which was to be one of the important themes of the early Hollywood years; and, especially, the famous notion of the "transfer" of guilt, which we see expressed here for the first time in the parallel editing showing on the one hand the blackmailer's desperate flight from the police and on the other, an admirable series of close-ups of the true murderess prostrate in remorse and prayer.

Blackmail was conceived and shot as a silent film. But the rapid extension of sound was already doing enormous harm to silent films no matter how good they were. John Maxwell and Alfred Hitchcock decided to sonorise the film. Hitch reshot the scene between Alice and the painter in a different way, adding a piano. Whereas in the silent version the painter (in a forward track) advances toward Alice, in the sound version he is singing softly at the piano, working himself up little by little before lunging at her. For the rest, Hitchcock merely added noises, music, and some dialogue. Since the Czech actress Anny Ondra, who played Alice, was unable to record her own dialogue, the English actress Joan Barry substituted for her.

The results were very strange. Hitchcock laughs until tears come into his eyes as he recalls the way in which the actors spoke the lines: "It looked as though they were reciting subtitles." It's true; yet the acting was by and large better than in the previous silents (excepting, of course, that of Ivor Novello). The performance, as conceived by Hitchcock, required sound. In this respect, the difference between the two versions is striking. Despite the mediocrity of the delivery, the sound version is better acted than the silent version. The stylization more or less consciously imposed on the actors by Hitchcock found its raison d'être with sound.

Moreover, Hitch demonstrated an overflowing imagination in his use of sound. For example, take the mixes alone. How can we help but admire the continuity a shriek achieves between the shot in which Alice suddenly finds herself face to face with the tramp lying in the position of the dead painter, and the following shot of the charwoman discovering the body![1] The director also makes remarkable use of sound in the breakfast sequence on the morning following the murder, when Alice sees on the table a breadknife similar to the one she had used in the killing. Just then, a woman in the room who has been talking about the story in the paper launches into a flood of words from which emerges only the single word *knife, knife*. The idea, an extremely original one at the time, was admirably exploited, and it remains effective even with today's more blasé filmgoer. But Hitchcock pushed the experiment further still and managed to make the inexpressible tangible with the help of a simple sound. Peter Noble cites with justified admiration the scene in which on the day following the crime Alice sees her fiancé-detective enter her father's shop. She reads on his face the suspicions that are troubling him (he has found Alice's glove in the studio), and the bell over the door resounds in her head like a knell.[2]

Blackmail was a triumphant success and reinforced Hitchcock's status. He was now the number one director in England. After he contributed a sketch for *Elstree Calling*, the first English musical, he was commissioned by John Maxwell to do the screen adaptation of Sean O'Casey's famous play *Juno and the Paycock* (1930).

[1]This idea was to be somewhat differently reworked in *The Thirty-Nine Steps*.
[2]Movie buffs will be interested to know that Ronald Neame was at the clapper board and Michael Powell was the still man.

As sometimes happens, a prestigious director was given the job of making a "prestige film." Hitchcock settled down to the job unenthusiastically, and what was at the time greeted as a great film now seems like something done as a boring assignment. The film is merely photographed theater, and it bears no relationship to the experiments that were to distinguish *Rope* or *Under Capricorn*. There is neither invention nor even a desire for invention in the shooting script. Though O'Casey's play is faithfully followed, the results are very boring. This minor tragedy set against a background of civil war, this attempt to capture the Irish Catholic soul, is treated by Hitchcock with sovereign disdain. Just as his film adaptation of *Easy Virtue* exposed Noel Coward's mechanics, so his *Juno and the Paycock* pitilessly underscored—this time perhaps unintentionally—the bathos and the weaknesses of Sean O'Casey's construction. However, though the images are without particular interest, the sound is given special attention: the creaking of the floor underfoot, intensive and grotesque use of accents, and a short burst of machinegun fire that makes the drowsy spectator jump in his seat. Only two scenes aroused Hitchcock's interest. The first is the one in which Juno and her friends gather around an old phonograph and break into some old folksongs in voices much the worse for drink. The characters' unbelievable idiocy evokes scenes in Ionesco. The other scene is the one in which the Sinn Feiners come to kidnap and slaughter the half-wit who has betrayed them.

Strangely enough, Sean O'Casey's Irish Catholic mystique in *Juno and the Paycock* strongly embarrassed Hitchcock, even though he himself is a Catholic. This fact is important. It provides a valuable clue to Hitchcock's feelings about the expression of religious problems on the screen. *The Ring, The Manxman,* and *Blackmail* are films of Catholic inspiration. The relations between people, the concept of the couple, of the family, of adultery—all contribute to the designation of Hitchcock as a Catholic auteur. But he refuses and will continue to refuse to sermonize, to proselytize—so much so that audiences were quickly to forget the essentially Catholic nature of his work. So much so that his films were to engender a complete misunderstanding about his intentions, since the spectator could not see beyond appearances.

It's easy to understand what shocked Hitchcock in Sean O'Casey's play. *Juno and the Paycock* was by no means free of proselytism—far from it. Hitchcock likes ambiguity, subtlety, mystery. There is nothing of this in O'Casey, who is all simplicity, all frankness, all robustness, and elementary to the very tip of his pen. The job Hitchcock had been given called for absolute fidelity; it was impossible to undertake the usual reconstitution, the usual polishing, impossible to make the story his own. Under these circumstances, the director carried out this assigned task as just that. Though one may admire his choice of actors (Sara Allgood, Edward Chapman), *Juno and the Paycock* is not an Alfred Hitchcock film.

Its success was nevertheless enormous, and O'Casey, enchanted, proposed a script on Hyde Park to the film-maker. Hitchcock rejected the temptation. He was in the midst of discussions with Clemence Dane and Helen Simpson—whose novel *Under Capricorn* he was later to film—about an eventual adaptation of their play *Enter Sir John*. O'Casey's script became a play, *Within the Gates*. Two months later, Hitch began work on a film adapted from *Enter Sir John,* which he entitled *Murder!* (1930).

Hitchcock's inventiveness, subtlety, and profundity in *Murder!* was as great as his boredom had been in *Juno*. The film has not only withstood the test of time, but it is one of his most successful—or, at any rate, one of the three best films of his English period along with *Rich and Strange* and *The Thirty-Nine Steps*. In fact, *Murder!* has several unexpected characters as well as a maturity, a seriousness, and a freedom of expression that are only rarely to be found in his films shot on British soil. More importantly, this film throws light on Hitchcock's future handling of thrillers. From this point of view, *Murder!* is an almost unique godsend. The plot belongs to the popular detective genre in which a murder is followed by an investigation and a final disclosure of the guilty party; there are no "compromises" because they are unnecessary; lastly, and most significant, its style is very varied, the tone passing skillfully from one register to another exactly as if Hitchcock, finally feeling himself in full possession of his powers, wanted to "put on film" the ensemble of his formal obsessions. A plot summary follows:

Diana, a young actress, is discovered unconscious alongside the body of one of her friends. She is accused of murder, tried, and eventually found guilty, in spite of the efforts of one juror, Sir John, a famous actor-manager who is persuaded of the innocence of the woman with whom he has fallen in love. He tries—in vain—to get from her some details of the murder, and indeed she seems to have a secret she is unwilling to reveal. Retracing the police investigation on his own, he ends by discovering the strange truth: the assassin is the accused woman's fiancé, who works in a circus, where he does a trapeze act disguised as a woman. Having overheard a conversation between Diana and the victim, he has killed the latter because she revealed to Diana that he was a half-breed.

Obviously, this is an absolutely classic detective plot, but it is heightened by a very important and characteristic detail: there is no doubt that the assassin's true secret is not that he is a half-breed in the ordinary sense but a sexual half-breed, a homosexual. Hitchcock makes no attempt to hide his intentions: he shows us many of the character's feminine tics (he pats his hair, studies himself in mirrors, pirouettes, becomes hysterical) and even shows him to us dressed as a woman! Once this is understood, the film is seen in an unexpected light: it is the first panel of a triptych that includes *Rope* and *Strangers on a Train,* a triptych that illustrates the problem of homosexuality from three points of view: moral in *Murder!,* realistic in *Rope,* and psychoanalytic in *Strangers on a Train.*

In *Murder!* the homosexual kills when he is unmasked. Unlike the protagonists of *Rope,* or Bruno Anthony (Robert Walker) in *Strangers on a Train,* he considers himself abnormal and is aware that his vice is a defect. But he is also incapable of loving, and he is interested only in escaping the consequences of his crime. When Hitchcock gets around to probing the problem of homosexuality in the two other films, we will become aware that his condemnation of homosexuality is justly based on the impossibility of true homosexual love: since this love is only an imitation, it is condemned to nonreciprocity. Diana loves the homosexual, since she allows herself to be convicted in his stead, but the homosexual doesn't love her, since he permits her to do so.

But the important qualities of *Murder!* derive from the purity of its direction. We have already noted its freedom of tone and style. The film opens with a long lateral track, punctuated by cries and the sound of footsteps, in which a black cat crosses the screen—an agonizing dolly that suggests the imminence of murder. Next come, unexpectedly, a series of squalid or burlesque observations: a big woman has trouble with her nightgown, a man can't pull up his window. Though the setting is London, there is nothing British about it. It recalls German expressionism and suggests Berlin. Later, this impression is furthered by the contrast between the minute realism of details and the stylization of whole scenes. The deliberation of the jury is presented without so much as a striking clock or an off-camera sound, but little by little the camera settles on the face of Sir John, around whom in turn appear the faces of the jurors arguing, giving their reasons, losing their tempers; the sound is intensified, the hubbub becomes infernal and completely unreal. Add to this the prison scene in which Sir John questions the woman he loves and who is going to be hanged, and everything—the framing, the lighting, and even the décor, which is reduced to a few essential lines—irresistibly evokes Murnau. First Griffith in *The Manxman* and now Murnau: Hitchcock acknowledges his masters.

But he also shows how he differs from them, and *Murder!* gives us a moment of marvelous Hitchcockian purity. Sir John is in his dressing gown in the bathroom. He sips a glass of old port and looks at himself in the mirror as he listens to the prelude to *Tristan and Isolde.* We "hear" the stream of thoughts on which he is being carried toward the imprisoned young woman. In this very long shot, just faintly embellished by a slight forward track, the

"Murder! (1930) has . . . a maturity, a seriousness, and a freedom of expression . . . only rarely to be found in his films shot on British soil." Sir John (Herbert Marshall) visits the scene of the crime. (PHOTO FROM BRITISH NATIONAL FILM ARCHIVE)

combination of *all* the visual and sound elements makes us literally feel, as though it were a caress, the slow and irresistible welling up of love in the character's heart. In addition, the choice of Herbert Marshall as the leading man was a stroke of genius. Like Ivor Novello, Marshall was a Hitchcock-type actor: unusual, seductive, intelligent. We will rediscover this character in the Robert Young of *The Secret Agent,* the Joseph Cotten of *Shadow of a Doubt,* the Cary Grant of *To Catch a Thief . . .* and, again, the Herbert Marshall of *Foreign Correspondent.*

Once more, Hitchcock shows his predeliction for the final "climax." In *Blackmail,* the British Museum sequence already contains a suggestion of the apocalyptic. Here the setting is a circus in which we follow the dizzying whirls of a trapeze artist in a tutu. The desire to conclude with a spectacular touch is not the only reason for this choice. As in certain moments in *Spellbound, Strangers on a Train,* or *To Catch a Thief,* the film leaves behind the earth to which it was strongly anchored by the minutiae of detail and launches into a world of vertigo and paroxysm.

The exceptional quality of *Murder!,* the considerable progress it revealed, and its more than respectable commercial success make it difficult to understand why Hitchcock next agreed to do a film based on John Galsworthy's play *The Skin Game* (1931). The only apparent reason would seem to be that Galsworthy's considerable literary reputation would provide Hitchcock with an opportunity to demonstrate the magnitude of his ambition. The play was bad and already dated, but perhaps Hitchcock thought he could "make something of it." If this was the case, he was soon brought down a peg, because *The Skin Game* is the worst film he has ever put his name to—a botched job in which the auteur seemed totally uninterested. There is no trace of stylization in the acting or of precision in the direction. On several occasions the movements of the actors, who are obviously doing whatever comes into their heads, catch the cameraman unprepared. As a result, we see either the beginnings of a camera movement that quickly comes to a halt, or the character stepping out of the frame while the camera wildly searches around for him in a sudden panic. It seems unlikely that this is a stylistic effect, especially since the film is completely devoid of all style. This imprecision on the part of the man who championed the use of storyboards indicates the film's unimportance in the work of Hitchcock, who doesn't care to be reminded of its existence. When he is, he immediately clamps his hands over

The disintegration of a marriage is studied in *Rich and Strange* (1932). Here Fred Hill (Henry Kendall) eyes a phony princess (Betty Amann) at a shipboard costume party. (PHOTO FROM BRITISH NATIONAL FILM ARCHIVE)

his eyes and ears in bitter contrition! So let us merely rescue from this dusty *The Skin Game* an amusing auction scene and a very beautiful shot in the last reel—and then let's pass over it as a film unworthy of its auteur.

Hitchcock owed himself a compensation—or at least that's the way *he* felt, for to his great surprise *The Skin Game* was very well received. He therefore next decided on a film to his own liking, one without concessions of any sort, a free and relaxed film. This was *Rich and Strange* (1932), which he still talks of with delight. It is his favorite film of the entire English period.

This preference is easily explained. Without resorting to the thriller arsenal, he deals here with a subject dear to him—the disintegration of a marriage. And he does so in a register that delights him—that of the notation of the comic, the strange. Hitchcock is not a fanatic about logic or probability, which he sees as just so many "compromises." He becomes more and more aware that he is not a "formalist" in the lofty sense of the word. He never hesitates to sacrifice everything—everything, including construction, logic, probability—to unity of tone. In *Rich and Strange* he takes a risk: the artist works without a net—without the net of the thriller plot with which he was often to protect himself in the future.

A letter announcing an inheritance allows a couple, Fred and Emily, to abandon a humdrum life. A long-dreamt-of voyage in the China Seas reveals their physical instability, in the form of seasickness, and their moral fragility, which is translated into the slow and progressive erosion of their relationship. The ship is wrecked and the door to their cabin is stuck. Water can be seen at the portholes. In the face of death, Emily and Fred swear eternal love and forgive one another their escapades. Several hours later they wake up on a deserted steamship now motionless on the sea. They are rescued by a junk manned by impassive Chinese and are present when one of them dies, thus learning how things are to be "borne"; they also witness the skinning of a cat, thereby learning the mystery of all things. Finally they return home, happy to regain the hell of everyday banality.

The tone of the work is the very image of its story. All of the first part, deliberately caricatural, deserves the adjective picaresque. Amusing and savage little scenes abound as the ship touches at Port Said, Suez, Colombo. The portrait is always a fierce one; the characters are puppets who seem to work autonomously. The auteur's position is clear at all times: a sovereign contempt, which we will come across again in more recent works such as *Rear Window*. This contempt hides the bitterness of the

The first part of *Number Seventeen* (1932), "a parody of horror films," takes place in an abandoned house. Ann Casson and John Stuart undergo a difficult moment. (PHOTO FROM BRITISH NATIONAL ARCHIVE)

moralist; the least surge of feeling on the part of his characters is enough to transform Hitchcock's contempt into affection.

The two pitiful protagonists of *Rich and Strange* experience this surge of feeling at the time of the shipwreck. The sequence in the cabin is certainly one of the most significant in all Hitchcock's work. The *absurdity* of this liquid and inexorable surface is better than words at portraying the unexpected abyss that the pointlessness of the cruise has created in the hearts of this pathetic couple. The extremely beautiful theme of the Unity of all things—one of the principal keys to all Hitchcock's great films—finds here, even more than in *The Manxman* and *Murder!,* an expression that is simultaneously savage and subtle. Hitchcock drives the lesson home in three significant scenes. First, the awakening of the enlaced couple in the cabin shows the return to fundamental unity and tenderly underscores the relativity of happiness. Then the arrival of the Chinese and the "incident" of the drowning (one of them, his ankle caught in a rope, dies as his companions look on impassively) remind those willing to understand that man's role is above all to accept his fate. Finally, it is on this junk in the middle of the China Seas that the English couple will find itself face to face with *mystery:* a cat is butchered by the Chinese and its skin stretched to dry, but it continues to take in the world with eyes that have lost none of their brilliance.

Hitchcock conceived this parable, which goes to the limit of the absurd, with a serene candor, and he introduces no trickery. The spectator who tries to latch on to its meaning by relating it to a defined genre will hopelessly lose his footing. There is no other way to see and admire *Rich and Strange* than purely and simply to experience it. Any other method is particularly dangerous because Hitchcock plays the game to the very end and does not permit himself the least explanation, the least commentary. The dialogue is reduced to its most simple form, to what is realistically necessary. The message—and there is a message—is carried by the images themselves.

Better still, Great Britain's most famous director indulged himself in the luxury and risk of making a film under nonstudio conditions. A good portion of *Rich and Strange* was shot in

"I hate this film, I hate this kind of film, and I have no feeling for it,"
Hitchcock stormed. Jessie Matthews and Esmond Knight in a scene from
Waltzes from Vienna (1933). (PHOTO FROM BRITISH NATIONAL ARCHIVE)

Marseilles, Port Said, or Colombo with a silent camera. A fifth of
the film has dialogue. The rest simply has a sound track and is
emphasized by a film score. This admirable daring was to serve as
an example to many film-makers confined to their studios and
handicapped by their big budgets.

Alas! Though the film was a marvelous artistic success, it was a
resounding commercial failure. British critics who had praised *The
Skin Game* to the skies (good God, why!) greeted *Rich and
Strange* sulkily and spoke of an abrupt decline. There was
evidently no appreciation of fantasy and audacity in English film
circles, and the movie didn't make a penny.

This failure unquestionably affected Hitchcock. There is something paradoxical about the fact that this popular film director

never managed to get his most daring, his most candid, works accepted. The failure of *Rich and Strange,* like the later failure of *Under Capricorn,* undoubtedly prevented him from continuing along a path that he nevertheless knew was promising. If we consider Hitchcock's overall career until now [1957], it immediately becomes apparent that all his films tend to blaze or consolidate a new trail, and that just when things are about to take off, a commercial failure checks his élan and forces him to look elsewhere. His most sincere works, such "pure films" as *The Manxman, Rich and Strange, Under Capricorn,* and most recently *The Wrong Man,* were culminating efforts, whereas to Hitchcock's way of thinking, they should have been points of departure.

Discouraged by the public's lack of understanding, after *Rich and Strange* Hitch tried instead to entertain this public. *Number Seventeen* (1932) provided the opportunity. The film is taken from a play which is itself adapted from a novel by Jefferson Farjeon, a prolix and popular writer who was halfway between the best and the worst, between John Buchan and Fergus Hume, between the good Edgar Wallace and the bad Edgar Wallace. The first part of the film retains the theatrical optic and takes place entirely in the stairway and on the landing of an abandoned house in which are an unidentified man, a tramp, an innocent English girl, three bandits, and an adventuress—all trying to get their hands on a necklace that passes from hand to hand, as though in a game of hunt-the-slipper. All of this is treated very broadly, as a parody of horror films. The various incidents succeed one another swiftly, and there is no opportunity to be bored.

The second part takes place on a freight train where everyone meets again. The three bandits suspect one another of being detectives in disguise. Everybody shoots at everybody else. The engineer is felled. As we all know, a train without an engineer goes mad. This train is no exception to that rule and smashes into a channel ferry patiently waiting for it at the quay. The unknown man confesses that he is a detective and the adventuress falls into his arms; they sneeze!

The amiable mystification of the first part here becomes deliriously and irresistibly comic. Fond of toys and models, Hitchcock makes use of electric trains and miniature buses for the chase sequence. *Number Seventeen* is a charming film to the extent that it shows us a grownup child playing with his favorite toys. But as diverting as this little film may be—it reveals Hitchcock as a Jiri Trnka [maker of puppet films] who is only half aware of himself—it is nevertheless an indication of the film-maker's confusion. It is a blow struck for no purpose. There is even cause to wonder if at the time Hitchcock was not considering abandoning the movies, or at least abandoning movie direction. Actually, his contract with British International was coming to an end. He was only the producer of the last film on which he worked for this firm. It was Benn Levy, his former scenario writer, who directed *Lord Camber's Ladies,* and it is no secret that Hitchcock never showed up on the set.

And so a period rich in remarkable works ended in a rout. Was Hitchcock looking for greater freedom? This is by no means certain. In any case, his only attempt at independent production ended in a real disaster. He agreed (one wonders why, and he himself has no idea) to adapt *Waltzes from Vienna* (1933), the Johann Strauss operetta, for the independent producer Tom Arnold. By the second week of shooting, the waltz had ceased to interest him. Perfectly aware that the film was dreadful, and having no intention of making it better, Hitchcock called together the actors, the technical crew, and the thousands of extras who had been assembled for the ball scene. Pointing to his director's chair, he announced: "I hate this film, I hate this kind of film, and I have no feeling for it. What I need is a drama, adventures!" The film was bad, and this time the execrable reviews were fully justified.

The Gaumont–British Period (1934–1937)

This slap in the face was salutary. Painstakingly, Hitchcock prepared a comeback. Remembering the immense success of

Blackmail, he decided to relapse into the suspense genre—after taking a thousand precautions. Thrillers only interested him to the extent that they were ambitious, even austere—like *Murder!*—but he knew something about them: they pleased audiences only to the extent that they were lively, not to say wild—like *Number Seventeen.* He therefore decided to work out a skillful dosage—50 percent *Murder!* and 50 percent *Number Seventeen*—in an attempt to develop a new genre, the intelligent espionage thriller. Lots of action, voyages, guilty looks, "gags," and an occasional unexpected probing of certain situations.

Charles Bennett, who had worked on *Blackmail,* suggested that he do a film on Peter the Painter, a London anarchist of the early 1900s who had tried to bring off an assassination in Albert Hall before he and his band were tracked to their lair by none other than Winston Churchill, who was then Home Secretary. Hitchcock eliminated Churchill, but thought the idea an excellent one and immediately set to work.

As can be seen, "sincerity" wasn't the essential element of *The Man Who Knew Too Much* (1934). But the genesis of this concoction shouldn't prevent us from recognizing its great merit. True, Hitchcock was looking for a recipe, but he wanted one that allowed a great deal of scope to the artist's talent, to his style. And actually, it isn't so much the recipe that bothers us as the proportions of the ingredients. In any case, this first version evidently failed to satisfy him, because twenty years later he felt the need to perfect the job.[1]

The plot is familiar. An English family vacationing in Saint Moritz hears the dying words of a secret agent: an assassination attempt will be made against a foreign dignitary in Albert Hall. The daughter of the couple is kidnapped in order to blackmail them into silence. Finally, the assassination fails and the band of spies is surrounded and then shot down.

The more recent version, which we will examine later, follows

[1]To "explain" the remake of this film in 1956, Hitch said that *The Man Who Knew Too Much* was the only one of his English films that Americans didn't know. We think he'll agree that this was a white lie, since on the contrary this film was one of the seven or eight of the English period that had a normal distribution in the USA.

In the first version of *The Man Who Knew Too Much* (1934), members of the Tabernacle of the Sun are strongly determined to prevent the protagonist from leaving and disclosing their plot. (PHOTO FROM BRITISH NATIONAL ARCHIVE)

the same general outline. But in the early version the implications are timidly expressed, the significant details stingily distributed. For example, the character of the leader of the band, the kidnapper, played by Peter Lorre, is almost incomprehensible.

In addition, in spite of its many good qualities, the first version of *The Man Who Knew Too Much* is somewhat irritating and unsatisfying, except perhaps for the final shoot-out (which is not repeated in the second version). This scene can stand comparison with the one in Fritz Lang's *Mabuse*, which seems to have inspired it. But the film's weaknesses didn't keep it from being a perfect strategic success—very much the contrary. Critics and public, having finally been given a Hitchcock that resembled their idea of him, applauded enthusiastically. They were only partly wrong, because the following year, Hitch, going back to the same principle, developed it to its highest point of perfection.

The plot of *The Thirty-Nine Steps* was freely adapted by Hitchcock and his wife, Alma Reville, and Charles Bennett from a famous espionage novel by John Buchan. Numerous changes were made (some details from another Buchan novel, *The Three Hostages,* were used), and they were all good ones.

As he leaves a music hall, a young Canadian, Richard Hannay, is approached by a woman who asks for protection. A secret agent working for England, she knows that her life is threatened by an occult and powerful espionage organization, "the thirty-nine steps." During the night, this young woman is stabbed, and as she dies she tells Hannay of the place in Scotland to which her mission was leading her. After many adventures, Hannay finds the spy, Jordan, who is disguised as a mild-mannered professor, and he denounces him to the police. Hannay is not believed, however, and is arrested for the woman's murder. He escapes and is recaptured by the men of "the thirty-nine steps," who also take along a young woman, Pamela, to whom he has confided his story. Another escape, this time in the company of Pamela, since they are chained to each other by handcuffs. They manage to learn that the document the spy wants will be turned over to him at the

The Thirty-Nine Steps (1935) established Hitchcock's international reputation. Professor Jordan (Godfrey Tearle) shows Hannay (Robert Donat) the deformed hand that distinguishes him. (PHOTO FROM BRITISH NATIONAL ARCHIVE)

London Palladium. Going there, they force Jordan to disclose himself by shooting at Mr. Memory, whose phenomenal memory has enabled him to learn a secret formula by heart. Mortally wounded, Mr. Memory unburdens himself of the weight on his mind by reciting the formula to the police before he dies.

What enchanted Hitchcock about this story is that it's a perfect example of the thriller plot in its pure state—so much so that it has as an essential characteristic the essence of every thriller. When adventures, whatever they may be, oppose two antagonistic forces defined in terms of Good and Evil, they necessarily imply a moral (cf. R. L. Stevenson). If thrillers generally mean nothing, it is because the antagonists are watered down, logically, or even psychologically. The difference between Graham Greene and Agatha Christie, let us say, is due to this factor. In *The Thirty-Nine Steps* the thriller theme is presented in its raw state. On the one side the hero, whose sole function it is to be the hero, and on the other side a mysterious and maleficent organization—"shadowy," to use Balzac's word—with a powerfully evocative name.

Given this, all a film-maker has to do is impose a style, a consistent and unswerving tone, and this story becomes a thriller allegory. Quite spontaneously, Hitchcock found the means by which to raise the level of the conflict and multiply the telltale signs of this requirement. When Professor Jordan lifts his hand and shows the stupefied Hannay the sign that distinguishes the great master of "the thirty-nine steps," this sign, in a twice repeated close-up, designates him as surely as would a pair of horns or cloven hooves. The idea is in itself very fine and more significant than it seems, for the sign is precisely an absence, a lack: Jordan has only four fingers. It is impossible not to recall the comparison of Professor Marrou, who defined human nature as "a dry sponge in which the holes are the image of Satan and the matter all that is not him." Interestingly enough, in borrowing a scenario detail (a book that stops the deadly bullet) from Fritz Lang's *Spies* (1928), Hitchcock converts it into his own and confers upon it a special meaning by making that book a Bible, which Hannay unknowingly carries over his heart.

As can be seen, the timidity and concessions of *The Man Who Knew Too Much* have been transformed into audacity—calculated, to be sure, but incisive. All the while conserving the famous dosage principle, all the while giving his film the appearance and form of a perfect espionage thriller, the director manages to express a certain number of ideas that are dear to him—ideas of which another example, one of the most extraordinary, can be found in the death of Mr. Memory. Here, in fact, Hitchcock shows us the mechanism of confession and how it works. Burdened with a bothersome and tormenting knowledge (it is absurd and ridiculous: an incomprehensible physics formula), Mr. Memory, after having recited it as though he were vomiting it up, dies saying, "I'm glad it's off my mind." In itself, of course, this underlying theme is not enough to give value to *The Thirty-Nine Steps,* but it adds a precious stone to the construction of the Hitchcockian universe outlined in his very first films. It also reinforces the astonishing formal qualities of the work.

Because here, too, Hitchcock triumphs. At his ease, sure of charming audiences, he multiplies the beauties. He is relaxed. The richness of the material is naturally complemented by the richness of the scenario and of the direction. Influences are assimilated, the personality flashes through. The atmosphere of a cheap London music hall is created in two shots. The truth is effortlessly born from a variety of picturesque details. The transitions seem self-generated. Each scene becomes a bravura piece, and beauty—the natural beauty of gestures and of things that the great Murnau knew so well how to create—bathes entire scenes, such as the meeting with the Scottish farmer and his wife or the episode with the sheep and the flight under the waterfall.

The Thirty-Nine Steps is without doubt Hitchcock's most famous English film. It is also the one that made his name known all over the world and got him his first offers from Hollywood. The concessions, inherent in the very principle of dosage, are sublimated in it by the perfection of its success. Here at last is the ambitious commercial film. But it should not be surprising that Hitchcock prefers *Rich and Strange,* into which he put himself more freely and certainly less calculatingly; sincerity is the only possible scale of value for a creator. Nevertheless, *The Thirty-Nine Steps* resolves for the first time—and if not for the last time, for a long time—the squaring of Alfred Joseph Hitchcock's personal circle.

Given this triumphant success—due in part, as he was well aware, to a misunderstanding—Hitchcock decided not to relapse but to continue along the same path. With *The Secret Agent* (1936) he tried to impose his perception of the world—to modify the dosage by increasing the proportion of sincerity—without, however, giving up the principle. He therefore now chose to adapt an episode from *Ashenden,* a novel by Somerset Maugham, a writer who is considered more "serious," more "literary," than good old John Buchan. For further insurance, he took as his scenario collaborator, in addition to the inevitable Charles Bennett, an American dialogue writer, Jesse Lasky, Jr. The scenario, as was to be true of all later ones, was constructed so that Hitchcock could find in it all the elements necessary to express what he had in mind. This formalist had arrived at the ideal point—he was never to stray from it—at which form finds the substance it needs.

Ashenden, an agent of the Intelligence Service, is sent to Switzerland during World War I to eliminate a spy whose identity he does not know. He is to be helped in his assignment by a professional assassin, a double agent, and by Elsa, an apprentice spy who will pass as his wife. Soon, all suspicions point to a tourist. Everything seems to fit, and it only remains to eliminate him, something the double agent undertakes to do. But there has been an error. The true spy, a charming and gracious young man, unmasks himself on the train returning to England. The train is bombarded and derailed; the spy, mortally wounded, cuts down the double agent before he himself dies.

This simple outline makes it easy to recognize a series of Hitchcockian themes: the presumed guilty man who is not guilty, the journey in a foreign land, etc. More remarkable still, since the character appears here for the first time, the mysterious spy, the traitor, the evil man, is no longer the unsettling Abbott of *The*

The train bearing Madeleine Carroll, John Gielgud, Robert Young, and Peter Lorre back to England is bombarded by British planes in *The Secret Agent* (1936), based on Maugham's *Ashenden*. (PHOTO FROM BRITISH NATIONAL ARCHIVE)

Man Who Knew Too Much or the cold Professor Jordan of *The Thirty-Nine Steps,* but a charming young man full of delicate attentions and as dangerous as he is sympathetic. It is the foreshadowing of an evil that is young and seductive, a theme which was to furnish the subject of so many films of the American period.

But these aren't the only qualities of *The Secret Agent.* It is seething with more gripping Hitchcockian traits. For example, there is the scene in the church to which Ashenden and the double agent go to contact the organist. As they reach the door, they hear the organ sounding a single note; when they get to the instrument, they discover that the organist has been murdered, and his body is pressing against the keyboard. There is also the scene in which a peaceful chocolate factory is suddenly shown to be an espionage center.

But *The Secret Agent* goes further still—perhaps too far. Hitchcock unhesitatingly makes use of one of his favorite methods: an abrupt change of tone. Here, as in *Rich and Strange,* the first part of the film is made up of "gags." In it, espionage skirts parody. Peter Lorre, as a factitious Mexican general and double agent, flirts with every woman he sees, and, for the sheer pleasure of it, amuses himself by terrorizing a little girl on a funicular. The impression is conveyed that these people are entertaining themselves by playing at spy and living a high life in a sumptuous Swiss hotel. The tragic error—the murder of the innocent suspect—brings about a sharp intervention of morality, conscience, bad conscience, in this parlor game. Though the double agent takes the matter lightly, Ashenden and the young woman fully recognize their responsibility. They understand that this error makes murderers of them, turns them into something similar, or almost so, to those they are hunting.

This awareness is expressed in their relationship. *He* must win back his self-esteem; *she* tries to restore his confidence. The two scenes in which we see this at work are in Hitchcock's best vein and represent his considerable skill with actors as unspontaneous as John Gielgud and Madeleine Carroll.

Despite all its qualities, despite the exceptional assurance of the direction, *The Secret Agent* is somewhat less satisfying than *The Thirty-Nine Steps.* It was impossible to modify the so-successful dosage of the previous film without unbalancing the work. In once more attempting to add more of himself, to raise the level of the conflict, Hitchcock unbalanced the harmony. However, the film enabled him to consolidate his position with Hollywood by

Sylvia Sidney and Oscar Homolka in a scene from *Sabotage* (1936). Hitchcock's free adaptation of Conrad's *The Secret Agent* allowed him to remain faithful to his own temperament. (PHOTO FROM BRITISH NATIONAL ARCHIVE)

demonstrating that he was a director of "international" status. It was to push this demonstration even further that he undertook *Sabotage* (1936) immediately thereafter.

This work is certainly unique in Hitchcock's career. Having found a subject of the type best suited to inspire him, he deliberately chose to use it in a film whose sole purpose was personal prestige. He went about it with great care. After having sifted the critical articles about him, the faults found with him, the praises showered on him, he created a second personality that completely corresponded with the idea others had of him. He was entirely aware that a film made in this manner would be academic, cold, and meretricious, but he also knew that it would open the way to a bright future.

Operation *Sabotage* was based on three pillars:

1) The choice of an author who was not only literary but this time "classic"—he chose Joseph Conrad.

2) The adaptation of this author with sufficient fidelity to prevent charges of betrayal, but with sufficient freedom so that it would at all times be possible to see that Hitchcock had remained faithful to his own temperament.

3) The direction of the film with such dazzling virtuosity that it would evoke the best of Hollywood without sacrificing a certain British chic.

In order to make sure that he hit the target, he signed up a famous American star who was also a fine actress (this would make it clear that he knew real talent when he saw it): Sylvia Sidney.

Of course, the ultimate trick would have been to top it all off by making an excellent film, but there was no point in being finicky this time around. What he had to do was hit hard and below the belt.

London is deprived of light by an act of sabotage. The saboteur, who cloaks his activity behind the mild-mannered appearance of a local movie-theater manager, lives with his wife and her young brother. He receives a new assignment: to place a bomb in the subway. The boy, obviously unaware of the nature of the package he's been given to carry, lingers in the streets, and is killed when the bomb explodes in a bus. The young wife suspects her husband, and the investigation turns her suspicions into certainty. She stabs her husband and flees. The police come to arrest the saboteur, but a providential explosion keeps the young woman's crime from being discovered. She is free to rebuild her life with a handsome police detective.

This story might have served to make a film as good as *Murder!* Hitchcock chose academicism. Polished, repolished, too polished to be honest, *Sabotage* was, of course, praised to the skies. It was the "psychological" film long expected of Hitchcock. The death of the little boy made all the intellectuals feel that they were

A production shot made during the filming of *Young and Innocent* (1937) shows the camera beginning its celebrated slow descent to frame the drummer's twitching eyes. (PHOTO FROM BRITISH NATIONAL ARCHIVE)

witnessing the absolute acme of audacity, whereas it must be acknowledged that Hitchcock had deliberately treated it very gingerly and made use of only one happy effect: the scene in which a toothpaste demonstrator delays the boy for a few precious minutes. Another much admired scene, that of the young wife's crime, makes use of a series of showy tricks that do not begin to compare with the original and powerful expressive devices used in *Blackmail* or *The Secret Agent.* Nevertheless, the basic approach was good: Hitchcock makes us feel that the wretch is aware that his wife is preparing to kill him (as in *Blackmail,* with a knife), and that remorse makes him resign himself to the role of victim. But he makes this too obvious, underscores his intentions with a disagreeable insistence. For the first and, happily, the last time in his career, Hitchcock condescends to the public instead of raising the public to him.

It would, however, be unfair not to draw attention to the very short and very fine sequence which follows that of the murder, when, as the young woman flees along the street, she thinks she sees her brother coming toward her. A breath of purest lyricism momentarily passes over the screen, and the spectator is seized by vertigo. Alas! We too soon afterward sink back into a "quality" film of the kind that probably gets that label from the fact that it is overly afraid of making mistakes. It's easy to understand why *Sabotage* is the Hitchcock film preferred by those who don't like Hitchcock.

The Gainsborough–Mayflower Period (1937–1939)

To compensate himself for *Sabotage,* which he had thought "necessary," Hitchcock undertook a film after his own heart. Since Michael Balcon was leaving Gaumont–British, Hitchcock decided to knock on the door of its little sister, Gainsborough, where he found a producer who didn't quibble and who gave him a free hand—Edward Black.

Having read a detective novel which he found "very, very bad,"

Josephine Tey's *A Shilling for Candles,* he decided to make a film
of it. Aided and abetted by Charles Bennett, he modified the
scenario until it lost all resemblance to the original and then gaily
launched himself into adventure.

Young and Innocent (1937) has many defects, but these defects
are more attractive than the glacial perfection of *Sabotage.* It's a
kind of "American Hitchcock film" ahead of its time, and those
features that still carry a whiff of English cinema are not the least
irritating things about it. The tramps, the countryside, and that
Victorian dining room seem out of place. In addition, the unlucky
hero bears an unfortunate resemblance to the French singer
Charles Trenet! But the film's qualities are so striking that *Young
and Innocent* nevertheless takes its place among the best films of
the English period.

During a stormy night, a man and a woman quarrel in a scene of
violence done in the masterful American manner. The scene ends
with a prolonged close-up of the man, whose right eye is twitching
in the lightning. The movie's plot then follows the usual pattern.
The woman is found dead on the beach, strangled with a raincoat
belt. Suspicion immediately centers on the owner of the raincoat,
who also happens to have been the dead woman's gigolo. Our
young scoundrel flees in order to find the murderer and is aided in
this undertaking by the daughter of the chief constable. The young
people pick up the trail of the raincoat and then discover the coat
itself on the back of a tramp, who was given it by the murderer.
The tramp helps the young man to identify the real assassin, who is
a blackfaced player in a tearoom orchestra, but who is spotted
thanks to the nervous twitch of his eyes.

This run-of-the-mill plot leaves Hitchcock all the time he needs
to linger over the peripheral details of his subject and create an
abundance of poetic, funny, or terrifying shots. There are, for
example, the scene in the loft of the old mill, where the young girl
brings the fugitive food; the scene in the marshaling yard, where
the two young lovers, clinging to each other, spend the night; the
children's party, at which an overly fond uncle plays the buffoon;
and the scene in an abandoned mine, where the ground gives way

under an old jalopy. In addition, *Young and Innocent* has the most beautiful forward track to be found in the history of film: the protagonists enter the ballroom of a fancy hotel in which the murderer is probably hiding; though the spectator has previously seen him, all he knows about him is that his eyes twitch. The camera, mounted on a crane, is some forty yards overhead and follows, in a short pan, the entry of the young people into the ballroom, at the far end of which one can see a black orchestra playing a number while couples move about the dance floor. The camera begins a slow, oblique descent, as if searching to frame the orchestra. It does frame it, and it continues to move forward until it takes in only a portion of the orchestra, then only three musicians, and finally only a single musician: the drummer. The camera comes closer still, until only the drummer's face is on the screen. The camera searches for his eyes, finds them, and isolates them. The eyes twitch.

Even the celebrated track shot onto the key in Ingrid Bergman's hand (*Notorious*) is less impressive than this one. In addition, *Young and Innocent* contains a very successful preliminary sketch of the family scenes in *Shadow of a Doubt:* we hear the same hubbub of conversation, a factor which tends to prove that when it comes to sound, Hitchcock owes less to Orson Welles than is generally believed. The film's only weak point, when it is compared to his American movies, or even to *Blackmail,* is that Hitchcock was not very inspired by his leading lady, Nova Pilbeam, whom he had already used as a child prodigy in *The Man Who Knew Too Much.* Just as Teresa Wright and Anny Ondra charm us, so Nova Pilbeam leaves us—and him—cold. Hitch's response to his actresses is very interesting. Some inspire him, others do not. In the first group are Lillian Hall-Davies, Anny Ondra, Madeleine Carroll (yes indeed!), Margaret Lockwood, Joan Fontaine, Carole Lombard, Teresa Wright, Tallulah Bankhead, Ingrid Bergman, Marlene Dietrich, Jane Wyman, Anne Baxter, Grace Kelly, Doris Day, Vera Miles. In the second, happily less numerous group, are Betty Balfour, Anne Grey, Jessie Matthews, Nova Pilbeam, Maureen O'Hara, Laraine Day, and Ruth Roman.

Dame May Whitty is rescued by Margaret Lockwood and Michael Redgrave in *The Lady Vanishes* (1938), an "exact summing up of the Gaumont-British series." (PHOTO FROM BRITISH NATIONAL ARCHIVE)

And finally came *The Lady Vanishes* (1938), which was also produced by Edward Black. Hitchcock felt this would be his last film in England. He had decided that immediately after finishing it he would accept one of the Hollywood offers, though he still didn't know which one. He wanted to end with a splash, to do something that would simultaneously be the product of four years of experimentation, a summary, and an end to a particular period. He chose to adapt an espionage novel by Ethel Lina White, *The Wheel Spins,* and assigned the scenario to the young team of Frank

Launder and Sidney Gilliat, modifying it with the help of his wife
during the actual filming.

The Balkans. In a mountain hotel are assembled the travelers of
a snowbound train. There are a series of comic incidents, amidst
which the murder of a guitarist goes unnoticed. The next day all
the travelers gather on the platform of the departing train. On
board, Iris, a young Englishwoman who is returning to London to
marry, begins a conversation with an old woman, Miss Froy. The
latter disappears, and with the exception of Iris, nobody seems to
have seen her. Aided by Gilbert, a young folkdance specialist with
whom she had had a run-in the previous night at the hotel, Iris sets
out to look for her in the various compartments. Another traveler,
Dr. Hartz, tries to persuade the young woman that she is suffering
from an hallucination and that Miss Froy does not exist. After a
series of tragi-comic incidents, Iris and Gilbert find the old
woman, who is actually a secret agent whom Hartz has been
assigned to eliminate. But their railway car is shunted off to a side
track and attacked. Miss Froy escapes into the woods while
Gilbert, to whom she has confided her secret, takes over the
controls of the engine and brings the train back onto the path to
safety. Everybody, including Miss Froy, meets up again safe and
sound in good old London.

The Lady Vanishes is almost an encyclopedia. It is the exact
summing up of the Gaumont–British series, and therefore requires
little commentary. Its early parts feature the models and mechanical cars that Hitch loves to play with. The actors are excellent, and
young Margaret Lockwood is certainly more beguiling than Nova
Pilbeam. Hitchcock is finally able to impose on the public that
two-tempo construction which had seemed so troublesome in Rich
and Strange and The Secret Agent. The allusions to current world
developments are biting, and the white handkerchief waved in
vain by one of the passengers, an antipathetic neutralist, cannot
fail to evoke Munich. The verve of Sidney Gilliat's dialogue in no
way submerges the director's personality. It's an excellent English
film, an excellent Hitchcock film.

Jamaica Inn (1939), a period film starring Charles Laughton, may in some ways be considered "a rough sketch for one of his later masterpieces, *Under Capricorn* (1949)." (PHOTO COURTESY OF MUSEUM OF MODERN ART)

Before leaving for America, Hitch received a tempting offer from Charles Laughton and Erich Pommer. The two men had just founded a producing company, Mayflower, and asked him to make a movie for them (with Laughton, naturally) of Daphne du Maurier's novel *Jamaica Inn.* He quickly accepted for two reasons: he wanted to direct Laughton, and one can understand why; and he wanted to accept the Hollywood contract offered him by David O. Selznick, provided that the latter, who had bought the rights to *Rebecca,* another Daphne du Maurier novel, would allow him to make a movie of it. To film *Jamaica Inn,* therefore, could only reinforce his position with Selznick.

Jamaica Inn is a period film (the action takes place at the end of the eighteenth century), a genre Hitchcock had not attempted since his sad experience with *Waltzes from Vienna.* He did not fall into the trap of historical reconstruction but focused instead on making a baroque and highly embellished work. This *Jamaica Inn* may be a rough sketch for one of his later masterpieces, *Under Capricorn* (1949).

The heroine is a young Irish girl, Mary, who goes to England to stay with her Aunt Patience, whose husband, Joss, is the owner of the Jamaica Inn, a disquieting hospice on the Cornish moors. On the way, Mary meets Sir Humphrey Pengaltan (Charles Laughton), a magistrate, who is greatly attracted to her but of whom she is instinctively mistrustful. Little by little, Mary becomes aware that Joss and his tavern provide a hideout for fearsome wreckers. Unaware that Sir Humphrey is their ringleader, she seeks refuge with him and witnesses the pillage of ships that have been wrecked after being lured onto the rocks. Fired by a desire to make Mary his own, Sir Humphrey does away with the innkeeper and his wife and flees with the young Irish girl, whom he forces to embark with him for France. Luckily, the police have been tipped off by a member of the force who has penetrated the gang, and they surround his ship just as it is about to lift anchor. Rather than surrender, the eccentric Sir Humphrey eludes capture by climbing the rigging and then commits suicide by throwing himself from the mast.

We were unable to resee this film, which has not been shown in France since 1945, but several sharp and entertaining images remain vivid in our memories: the heroine taking down a hanged man, a pirate whistling a mazurka as he wipes his bloody cutlass on his shirt, the carriole rolling through the brush, and above all Sir Humphrey's fall onto the deck. Twenty years before Max Ophuls, the camera plunges from atop a mast and seems to crash against the ground: the final stunt in a minor work that is a little too much like its artificial and bizarre protagonist, admirably played by the innately and inventively prodigious Charles Laughton in a role actors dream about.

2

THE AMERICAN PERIOD (1): WITH SELZNICK

The negotiations with Hollywood begun in 1936 ended in 1939. The chosen one was David O. Selznick, who had just produced *Gone with the Wind.* As Hitchcock had foreseen, Selznick promised him the direction of Daphne du Maurier's novel *Rebecca,* and that promise determined his decision. At the beginning of the summer, he set sail with his wife, his daughter, and his secretary, Joan Harrison. Two months later shooting began.

The scenario of *Rebecca* is signed by Robert Sherwood, the author of *The Petrified Forest,* and Joan Harrison. The presence of this latter name shows that Hitchcock had not abandoned the good habit of keeping close track of the development of his scenarios. As we have seen, he had no prejudices about the origins of his film plots. Daphne du Maurier's novel, the literary value of which is dubious, had the advantage of being a bestseller. The adaptation was faithful because it was important that readers not be disappointed. The story was merely tightened up, and very few new scenes were added: for example, the home movies session, which has the triple advantage of summing up the honeymoon, underscoring Maxim's strange reactions, and being a comedy festival. The story, however, remains the same. A young woman, a lady's companion, marries a handsome aristocrat—a mysterious man, tormented by the memory of his first wife, that Rebecca of the haunting absence—and comes into conflict with his housekeeper, who remains devoted to the memory of the deceased. But though the story remains the same, the tone is different. The gossipy and somewhat affected novel has become a fairytale thriller, modern and disquieting. Even as he scrupulously respects the letter, Hitchcock manufactures the spirit. Every creator goes through a stage of "crystalization" in which his universe finally takes shape. In his best English films, Hitchcock was in search of something he could not completely grasp; *The Ring, The Manxman, Blackmail, Murder!, Rich and Strange, The Thirty-Nine Steps,* and *The Lady Vanishes* are admirable youthful works. *Rebecca* is something else again: the first manifestation of a mature talent. It is not at all surprising that this maturity coincided with Hitchcock's arrival in America: leaving his usual surroundings acted as a catalyst.

With *Rebecca,* the "Hitchcock touch," which has previously been merely a distinguishing feature, becomes a vision of the world. Spontaneity submits to a system. This is a critical moment for an artist, for he must not develop tics, a pedagogical fury. Hitchcock was to avoid these traps. From now on, the two poles of his future work—because we can now talk of a body of *work*—are clear. One is fascination, moral captation—in other words, depersonalization, schism: in psychoanalytic terms, schizophrenia; in philosophic terms, amoralism; in Baudelairean terms, the assumption of evil, damnation. The other pole is its opposite: knowledge—or, more exactly, reknowledge—of self, unity of being, acceptance, confession, absolute communion. As the heroine of *Rebecca* explains, her father always painted the same tree because he felt that when an artist has found his subject, that is all he wants to paint. And indeed the work of our artist will henceforth never stray from its path.

However, this work of purification was not to progress without some stumbling and fumbling, of which there are numerous examples in the first films of the American period. Quite naturally, *Rebecca* is part of the settling-in process. The least assured of Hitchcock's great films, it contains on a "take it or leave it" basis things that Hitchcock was later either to take or leave. The character of the housekeeper, Mrs. Danvers, is less subtle than

Hitchcock's American debut was made with *Rebecca* (1940), which starred Joan Fontaine and Laurence Olivier. Though the film is faithful to the bestselling novel, the tone is different. (PHOTO COURTESY OF MUSEUM OF MODERN ART)

that of Milly in *Under Capricorn*. George Barnes's photography lacks the brio the director was later able to obtain from Joseph Valentine and Robert Burks. The shooting script itself is a bit too languidly graceful, and some of the camera movements are too precious. On the other hand, *Rebecca* contains the beginnings of, or the rough sketch for, many elements that were to be developed and refined in later works—for example, the stylization of the acting and the actors based on the relationship between the mobility of one face and the fixed impassiveness of the other, a stylization that was to achieve perfection in *Notorious,* for example, the mobile close-up, already made use of during the

English period but henceforth to be systematically employed to express fragility, instability. Actually, this is combined in *Rebecca* with a variation of focusing such as William Wyler was to use in *The Little Foxes;* but Hitchcock was quickly to abandon this latter method and in his later works use mobile close-ups only against a uniformly soft background—as is logical.

But the new note is especially to be found in the direction of the actors. In Hollywood, Hitchcock found players who were very different from those of the English studios. There was a greater selection, and henceforth all his films were to be acted to perfection; the result was his reputation as a wonderful director of actors. Yet everybody who has worked with him gets the feeling that he directs them only in relation to camera movements. Let's not be fooled: their liberty is only superficial, so much so that we will rediscover not only the same tone but the same mannerisms in actors as different as George Sanders in *Rebecca* and Robert Walker in *Strangers on a Train:* the same astonished eyebrows, the same sulking pout, the same half-homosexual, half-childish affectations. As for Joan Fontaine, this was her best performance. She was one of two great Hitchcockian leading ladies and inspired her director just as Ingrid Bergman was to a few years later.

Rebecca won the Oscar for the Best Film of the Year, and Hitchcock's services were in demand at most of the big studios. This was exactly what Selznick had hoped for, since he made it a principle to get film-makers and actors under contract with a view toward renting them out right and left. As a matter of fact, during his seven-year "exclusive" contract with Selznick, Hitchcock made only three films for him—*Rebecca, Spellbound,* and *The Paradine Case.* It was thus Walter Wanger who produced Hitchcock's next film at the beginning of 1940: *Foreign Correspondent.*

Dr. Goebbels considered *Foreign Correspondent* a remarkable and very dangerous film. Hitch, who is ordinarily not at all a "committed" auteur, made an exception where Nazism was concerned. *The Lady Vanishes, Foreign Correspondent, Lifeboat, Notorious,* and *Rope* are all, to a certain extent, political films.

Shortly before World War II breaks out, an American journalist, Jones, is sent to Europe to "analyze the situation." He meets a highly placed Dutch official who knows the secret of a treaty the Nazis are determined to discover at any price. They therefore kidnap him and kill a sosie. Jones discovers the truth, sets out to find the Dutchman, and tries to shake off the spies who are on his trail. From the land of windmills we go to England. Jones is accompanied on his flight by a young Englishwoman named Carol Fisher (Laraine Day), who brings him to her father. The president of a pacifist organization, Fisher is actually in league with the Nazis, and he provides the journalist with a bodyguard who is really a killer. (Luckily, he is a very inept one, and in a scene rich in suspense it is he himself who will be launched into the air from the top of a tower.) Several action-filled, comical, or cruel mishaps follow, and the tone is reminiscent of *The Thirty-Nine Steps*. Mention should be made of the flight, in a dressing gown, across the rooftops, and of its unexpected termination at a cocktail party; the scene in the country inn in which the young woman suspects the reporter of libertine intentions that are not quite what he has in mind; the torture scene in which the victim's shrieks are masked by jazz music, etc.

The Dutchman refuses to talk. Fisher will be unmasked, but on the day war is declared he will manage to catch a plane for America, with Jones sitting a few seats behind him. The plane is attacked by Germans and plummets into the sea. Fisher sacrifices himself in order to save his daughter. The survivors are picked up, and in spite of the captain's prohibition, Jones finds a clever way of telephoning his story to the paper. We later see him in London, broadcasting condemnations of the German bombardments to his fellow Americans.

Though the spirit and the composition (a series of sketches) are similar to those of *The Thirty-Nine Steps,* the direction is richer, more brilliant. The technical expertise of Hollywood was a precious boon to Hitchcock. For example, in England he would never have been able to film with the same brilliance the assassination scene in which we watch the murderer cleave a path through a sea of bowler hats and umbrellas. Hitch gives up aural and visual tricks—fades on identical noises or gestures, close-ups of deadly objects—that were unjustly seen as the basis for his reputation. Since he is no longer the prisoner of a bestseller, his language is more relaxed, more varied, than in *Rebecca*. Fisher, the philanthropic spy played by Herbert Marshall, is a typical Hitchcock character: he is the link between Professor Jordan in *The Thirty-Nine Steps* and Uncle Charlie in *Shadow of a Doubt*. He has the respectable but troubling mask of the former (the missing finger is replaced by a limp), and he has the elegance and corruption of the protagonist of the latter. It is this character that Hitchcock has polished up most carefully: Fisher incarnates the idea of the identification of the forces of Evil—in the demonological sense of the term—with Nazism. As we have noted, this theme is later to be reworked; here the approach is still a cautious one.

The next film belongs to a very different genre: American comedy as it was done before the war by Leo McCarey and Frank Capra. When Norman Krasna suggested to Hitch that he direct one of the comedies he had just sold RKO, the "Master of Suspense" accepted with pleasure. He went about the problem very seriously, keeping *Champagne* in mind, to some extent, but especially *Rich and Strange*. The result was quite curious. Hitch did not want to follow the usual technique of the genre, a technique based on simplicity and speed; only the acting style of the performers was to remain faithful to the tradition. Besides, the actors—Robert Montgomery and Carole Lombard—were experienced and excellent hands at comedy. They had already played the story of Mr. and Mrs. Smith many times. Hitchcock, who knows how to respect the skills of specialists, made no attempt to impose another style. Instead, he focused all his attention on the direction, which he wanted to be very characteristic of his personality.

The originality of the form is obvious from the very first scene. A slow panoramic dolly shot shows a bedroom in disorder: clothes and various other objects are piled on the floor or draped over the furniture. The camera stops a second in front of a bed from which the top of a woman's head emerges. The camera moves forward,

Though ordinarily not a "committed" film-maker, Hitch made an exception where Nazism was concerned. George Sanders, Joel McCrea and Laraine Day in *Foreign Correspondent* (1940). (PHOTO COURTESY OF MUSEUM OF MODERN ART)

In *Mr. and Mrs. Smith* (1941), starring Carole Lombard and Robert Montgomery, the "Master of Suspense" tried his hand at prewar American comedy as done by Leo McCarey and Frank Capra. (PHOTO COURTESY OF MUSEUM OF MODERN ART)

an eye appears, and then Carole Lombard's face. The slowness of this first shot is a radical departure from the reigning laws of American comedy. It conveys a sort of anxiety, and might just as well be used to begin a "suspense" film. The rest of the movie follows the same principle: all the scenes are shot from a subjective point of view. On several occasions we even witness attempts at a "subjective" camera. This forced identification with the character undercuts the laughter. Generally speaking, American comedy gets its effects from the assumption of objective observation: it is a report on madness. Here, we are accomplices of the characters. The laughter, when it does arise, abruptly shrivels up: the "gag" is not funny to the person at whose expense it is carried out. The only times we laugh in *Mr. and Mrs. Smith* (and even then not without some uneasiness) are those moments in which there is an abrupt shift from one subjectivity to another. Let's take the following example.

Their marriage having been annulled for technical reasons, Mr. and Mrs. Smith have decided to test their love by remaining single. Mr. Smith, who is dying of boredom, has already spotted his wife in the company of attentive gentlemen, and he is gnawed by jealousy. He lets one of his friends talk him into going to a restaurant. Both men are accompanied by two incredible floozies. No sooner have they sat down but Smith sees his wife and her boyfriend. Ashamed of being seen in such low company, he spots a young and beautiful woman sitting by herself at a neighboring table and pretends to be talking to her, as though she were with him. He gleefully observes that at the other end of the restaurant his wife is becoming upset. Just as he's about to glory in his victory, he sneezes, and one of the floozies quickly forces him to lie back on the table as a therapeutic measure. At this, Mrs. Smith bursts out laughing. So do we . . . During the first part of the scene, we have shared Smith's embarrassment and then his triumph. After the sneeze, we find ourselves on the other side of the fence, with Mrs. Smith. This leap from one "subjectivity" to another sparks laughter, but it is not cathartic laughter since we feel that we are mocking ourselves.

Mr. and Mrs. Smith does contain effects of pure comedy—for

Cary Grant and Joan Fontaine were featured in *Suspicion* (1941), in which a young woman becomes convinced that the charming man she had married is a gambler, a rake, and a murderer. (PHOTO COURTESY OF MUSEUM OF MODERN ART)

example, the final image in which Carole Lombard's skis rise to form a screen between the camera and the kiss she and her husband are exchanging—but these "gags," typical of American comedy, lack sparkle. On the other hand, the best moments—and we recognize in them the auteur of *Rich and Strange*—are those in which there is a "switch to the serious": for example, the anniversary dinner during which the couple vainly try to recapture the magic of their first dates together. The new restaurant owner watches them hostilely while they eat their favorite dish, a failure, in an agonizing silence . . . As in the shipwreck scene of *Rich and Strange,* the sense of the disintegration of love becomes almost unbearable.

Despite its uncertain success, this attempt at subjective direction had enchanted Hitchcock. He cast about for a subject that would allow him to carry his experiments further, and he chose a novel by Francis Iles, *Before the Fact,* which had been extremely popular three years earlier. This time Hitchcock did not feel constrained to absolute fidelity: for the first time he was coproducer of his film. With the help of Samson Raphaelson, Joan Harrison, and Alma Reville (a family operation!) he drew from *Before the Fact* the film *Suspicion* (1941).

The adaptation was such a strange departure from the novel that the critics cried foul. Francis Iles told the story of a young girl of English county society who falls in love with and marries a charming young man who is unfortunately a rake, a gambler, and a thief. Eventually, she becomes convinced that he is also a murderer. Worse yet, that he is planning to murder her. Because of her love for him, she determines to drink a glass of poisoned milk, thus becoming an accomplice in her own murder "before the fact." The situation is strong but artificial, and there is every reason to believe that it was only for that final scene that the novelist wrote his book. As for Hitchcock, he chose the novel not for that final scene but rather despite it. In the film, the young woman does not drink the glass of milk, and the glass of milk is not poisoned. The subject is no longer "how a woman drinks a glass of milk which she knows to be poisoned," but "how the gimlet of suspicion perforates the unity of a couple." Isn't this the same denouement? Of course not; it's not the same story! "Suspicion" is actually one of the favorite themes of the man who made *Rebecca,* so much so that there is not one of his films in which it does not play some role. In a manner of speaking, it is the psychological equivalent of that idea of "exchange," the moral aspect of which we will examine further on. We can even say that we are dealing with a privileged cinematic motif. In any case, it is by means of this motif that Hitchcock achieves an expression of the pure relation of soul to soul, that he pierces the protective screen of behavior, that he goes from the exterior to the interior, from the objective to the subjective. The somewhat cursory attempts at "subjectivity" find a much richer field of experimentation here.

The entire first part is a charming love story that moves along to the tune of a waltz. At no time does the spectator find it difficult to accept Joan Fontaine and Cary Grant as two attractive people, made for each other and in love. When suspicion insinuates itself, the tone changes—and so does the style. The narrator's point of view, which has until then been objective, becomes identified with that of the young woman: Cary Grant's behavior begins to seem more and more enigmatic, even though his performance has in no way changed. We remain in doubt, just as the heroine does. It might even be said, just as she *wants* to remain in doubt. If she does not drink the glass of milk, it is because what she fears most is being forced to renounce suspicion (and this is the proof, by way of the absurd, that the milk was *not* poisoned). She feeds on this suspicion like a vampire; she wants to wallow in the failure of her love.

In the very last scene, we see the suspicion dissipated, the husband exonerate himself entirely, and the young woman get back into the car she fled when she thought that the pseudo-criminal was getting ready to push her out of the incompletely closed door. But the spectator has seen the evidence, and doubt can still remain in his mind: sure of his claim to objectivity, he refuses to admit that he was mistaken and accuses the auteur of trifling, of being dishonest. Before *Suspicion,* whatever reservations one had about Hitchcock were essentially flattering. It was said: "He's wasting his time and his great talent on stories that are not worthy of him." After *Suspicion,* it would be said: "He shows his limitations. He's only a shallow virtuoso, a technician and not a true auteur." We have already had occasion—and we will again, for such is the purpose of this study—to reply to these accusations. The fact is that they once more obliged our film-maker to change registers, at least temporarily. Having read that his chase films of the English period were sorely missed, he decided to develop a fast-paced scenario based on an idea furnished him by his old confederate, Charles Bennett. Like a good businessman, Selznick sold it, for a considerable sum, to Frank Lloyd and Jack Skirball, who were then Universal producers, and for an equally consider-able sum he rented them the services of the auteur. And that was how Alfred Hitchcock came to make *Saboteur* (1942).

The principle behind this film was simple. Using an outline familiar to him—the innocent man unjustly accused and being pursued while he himself is pursuing the true criminals—Hitchcock decided to give us a potpourri of his English work, returning to certain features and elaborating them to the point of exaggeration, multiplying the allusions and the knowing winks. The point of departure is German espionage in the United States. A young warplant employee is accused of an act of sabotage which he has obviously not committed. He escapes from the police and pursues across the country the true guilty party, whose name, Fry, he has accidentally learned.

　　The action begins in California and ends in New York at the top of the Statue of Liberty, where the hero catches up with the mysterious Fry. This story, the extravagance of which is obvious, is put together with architectural skill: the gears mesh smoothly; the scenes dovetail into one another with absolute precision. Geo-graphic and ethnographic details, as well as local accents, are carefully noted. On the other hand, the direction is less sumptuous than that of *Foreign Correspondent,* but this only brings out the resemblance to an English film. Among the innumerable and obvious references, we cite the handcuffs and the bridge, which recall *The Thirty-Nine Steps;* the movie-theater sequence—in

The elusive Fry (Norman Lloyd) dangles from the torch of the Statue of Liberty as the hero of *Saboteur* (1942), Robert Cummings, tries in vain to reach him. (PHOTO COURTESY OF MUSEUM OF MODERN ART)

which Fry, pursued by the police, fires into the audience, while on the screen one of the characters is also firing—evokes the best scene in *Sabotage;* the charity ball, at which the hero and his companion are endangered by the spies while the crowd remains unaware, recalls the chapel in *The Man Who Knew Too Much;* and Fry's fall from the top of the Statue of Liberty, Charles Laughton's plunge at the end of *Jamaica Inn*. A brilliant satire of the spy mania, an amusing self-parody, *Saboteur* is only—and only claims to be—an entertainment. It all takes place as though Hitchcock had wanted to conclude a phase once and for all, and to point up the superficiality of the notions held about him by critics and public alike. The hero of the film tells a blind pianist that when he was young he played the triangle but had to give it up. To which the blind man replies that he was wrong to do so, that the triangle is a noble instrument. We like to think that this is an allusion to *The Manxman,* the failure of which forced Hitchcock to give up that noble dramatic instrument known as the "triangle." He was not to attempt it again until *Under Capricorn.*

Hitch had been right. Given the enormous success of *Saboteur,* Jack Skirball proposed that he make a film of his own choosing. He therefore unearthed a story by Gordon McDonnell and obtained the collaboration of two good writers, Sally Benson and Thornton Wilder. Thus was born *Shadow of a Doubt* (1943). The exterior shots were filmed in a small California town, just as two years earlier Jean Renoir had filmed *Swamp Water* in Georgia. The director attached major importance to the accuracy of the setting.

The plot is as follows: Charlie Oakley (Joseph Cotten) supports himself by charming and then murdering rich widows. Suspected by the police, he takes refuge in Santa Rosa with his sister's family. He is welcomed like the prodigal son. His niece and godchild (Teresa Wright), also called Charlie, greatly admires him. But little by little she becomes suspicious, and her suspicion is fed by a detective assigned to keep an eye on her uncle: according to the police, the murderer can only be either Uncle Charlie or another

In *Shadow of a Doubt* (1943), Uncle Charlie (Joseph Cotten), who supports himself by charming and murdering rich widows, takes refuge in a small town with his sister (Patricia Collinge) and her family. (PHOTO COURTESY OF MUSEUM OF MODERN ART)

suspect in the East. The latter, cut down by an airplane propeller just as he is about to be arrested, is wrongly accepted as the true guilty party. The case is closed, but Charlie, the niece, has by this time discovered the truth. She is terrified by her uncle's firm decision to settle down in the little town. Confronting him, she begs him to leave. He refuses, and knowing that she is in love with the detective, makes two attempts to eliminate her. Finally he flees, and during the course of a third attempt at murder, he dies under the wheels of a train. He is given a lavish funeral and an eloquent eulogy, during which Charlie and her boyfriend exchange whispered expressions of astonishment that the world can engender such monsters. As it happens, in his youth Uncle Charlie had been the victim of an accident, but his cynic's faith is presented by both him and the film-maker as a possible philosophy of life.

The tie uniting Charlie and her uncle is clearly indicated all during the film. The criminal and his niece not only have the same name, but they understand each other by a sort of telepathy. In addition, their characters are antithetical: Charlie is innocence, and Uncle Charlie, duplicity. She has the radiance of purity, he exercises an almost Mephistophelian charm over people. Charlie can therefore be seen as a single being in two different persons: the uncle, a man who is damned; the niece, an angel. It is almost impossible to see this work as only an ingenious example of a psychological thriller. The very structure of the scenario, the deliberate versification of the direction, preclude this. Everything in this film depends on the principle of rhyme. There is probably not one moment in it that does not somewhere have its double, its reflection. Or, if you prefer, let us say with François Truffaut, from whom we borrow these examples, that *Shadow of a Doubt* is based on the number two:

1. a) New York. We see Uncle Charlie, fully clothed, stretched on the bed. His head is on the right of the screen.

   b) California. Charlie, the niece, is stretched on a bed, fully clothed. The position is symmetrical—a mirror image of her uncle's.

2. a) Charlie goes to send her uncle a telegram.

   b) She finds waiting for her a telegram from her uncle.

3. a) The detective admits to Charlie that he is keeping an eye on her uncle, but he adds that

   b) Another detective is keeping an eye on another suspect at the other end of the country.

4. a) The detective announces that the suspect in the East is dead, cut down by a propeller.

   b) Uncle Charlie dies, cut down by a train.

In addition, *Shadow of a Doubt* contains two church scenes, two scenes in a garage, two police visits to the house, two scenes of meals, and two attempts at murder. Finally, the director will alternately bestow the same framing shots and the same camera movements on the uncle and the niece: two extraordinary close-ups of backs, two forward tracks, two low-angle shots, etc . . . But the flavor and the precision of the details are completely matched by the rigor of the architecture. Sound is used in the manner of Orson Welles (and that of *Young and Innocent*): the characters interrupt one another in the middle of a cue, they raise their voices to be heard, or they both speak at the same time.

All this, as well as the observation of a thousand realistic details, accentuates the film's documentary quality. People go about their business with the simplicity of provincials, the exuberance of American westerners. In this everyday context, the presence of a criminal makes for an uneasiness that Hitchcock enjoys heightening: for him, the extraordinary is only a means of making the ordinary more ordinary, and vice versa. We do have some reservations about the secondary characters—the officious little sister, the imbecile father, the neighbor who is fascinated by problems in detection; the entrances of all are funny, but the caricature lacks variety. These defects are probably due to the collaboration of Thornton Wilder, the author of *Our Town*.

We will limit ourselves to pointing out the finest aspect of this film, one of its auteur's favorites. This is the moral concept of "exchange," which is the main support of this construction and without which it would collapse like a house of cards. We have already met this matrix-idea of the Hitchcockian system along the way, and we will come across it more and more frequently. The seductive Uncle Charlie will have as cousins the Brandon of *Rope* and the Bruno Anthony of *Strangers on a Train;* his sophisms prefigure their sophisms. In this case, however, the presence of a true "transfer of guilt" initially escapes us: the young girl does not feel guilty and does not behave like a guilty person. But let us remember the uncle's point of view. "The world," he says, "is a foul sty." It is the world that he charges with the responsibility he is unwilling to assume, and the opprobrium with which he covers it splashes onto the soul, previously pure, of his niece, who is also part of that world. It is also the world that will be accused in the last bit of dialogue, this time between Charlie and her fiancé: Why do such monstrous beings exist? they ask. It is with the discovery of the innate defect of the universe—of the problem of Evil, philosophers would say—that the innocent simultaneously loses his innocence.

Shadow of a Doubt was a brilliant success. Continuing his round of the studios under the aegis of Selznick, Hitchcock next undertook to make for Fox a film whose action takes place entirely in a lifeboat: *Lifeboat* (1943). He chose as his producer Kenneth MacGowan, the publisher of *Hollywood Quarterly*. He explained his idea to John Steinbeck, who wrote a twenty-page treatment, and he himself worked on the adaptation with the help of Jo Swerling, who signed the screenplay.

We might as well confess that the beginning of the film inspires serious doubts. The theme of "shipwreck," which consists of temporarily returning a few human specimens—coming from different layers of society, or having opposing views—to a primitive level, is fraught with clichés. Hermetically sealed off from the world, the characters will revert to type in spite of themselves and therefore seem exaggeratedly stereotypical. Any attempt by the director to introduce nuances will only make the harshness of the basic characteristic more obvious.

A liner has just been torpedoed by a German submarine. Into the lifeboat we see clambering in turn a woman Journalist (the capitals are deliberate), a communistic Engineer, an Industrialist, a Sailor, a Black—who is a steward and a good Christian—a pretty Nurse, and an Englishwoman carrying her dead child. The director and the scenario writer naturally make use of the situation's picturesque aspects. But there is one element that should merit the most attention: the element of the sea. However, though Hitchcock is so often skillful in making use of both natural and artificial settings, he is strangely stilted here. His studio ocean in no way compares with the wild and magnificent one in the last part of *Foreign Correspondent*. There's no point in looking for the poetry of adventure here: we are in the presence of a spare moral tale.

But the moral of the fable, since fable it is, is less simplistic than one might have feared. The addition of a new ingredient heightens the enticing odor of the lazily simmering stew. A final castaway appears: a German (once more with a capital G), a crew member of the submarine that had torpedoed the liner. And since this is very much a fable, the new arrival, seductive in his own way, symbolizes the temptation of that Evil whose face is familiar to us. Hitch suddenly changes hats. Instead of a psychologist, he becomes a moralist. The Nazi will be the catalyst of the reaction: his presence will be enough to reveal the latent malaise. What's called for now is not chatter but action. And which of us acts well?

Where is crime? where is righteousness? Where is the truth? where is error? It soon becomes evident that the German means to bring the boat to a safe harbor—to a safe German harbor. The problem is complicated by the fact that he is the only one who knows anything about navigation. Should he be thrown over-board? No, says the Christian Black. Yes, says the atheistic Engineer. But are the reasons of either all that pure? Isn't the one acting out of fear, the other out of presumption? Under the rumble of the words hide suspect motivations: we are not deceived. Finally the Boche, caught red-handed in crime, is tossed overboard; but this execution is cowardly, ignoble, and the women who flutter about in the background of the scuffle are not spared. Hitchcock has caught a whiff of the unpleasantness of collective halitosis, and he makes one of his usual rapier thrusts.

In the final minutes of the film a German ship appears, and as the castaways watch, another ship, an American one, sends it to the bottom of the sea. A new Nazi sailor bobs up against the lifeboat. As the castaways prepare to haul him aboard, he points a pistol at them; they disarm him, they hesitate, and they finally pull him into the boat. The film ends on a rather enigmatic note: What's to be done with these people? Only the dead can tell us.

Hitchcock probably wanted to conserve both the anti-Nazi character of this film and a less circumstantial philosophy: "Judge not." A generous maxim of which we are presented here with only the disdainful obverse: "You do not have the right to judge."

The humor of the detail is extremely biting, and a cascade of acid observations contribute to the general moral of the tale. With cruel insistence, Hitchcock shows the Journalist successively surrendering to the sea her camera, her mink, and her typewriter, and finally using her bracelet as fishbait. (She will keep only her lipstick.) An idyl will be sketched in—naked feet caressing one another with a hint of obscenity. The grotesque postures of the protagonists rob them even of that beauty lent by the etching of

A final castaway appears in *Lifeboat* (1943)—the captain (Walter Slezak) of the German submarine which sank their freighter. John Hodiak, Tallulah Bankhead, Henry Hull, Heather Angel, and Mary Anderson debate his fate. (PHOTO COURTESY OF MUSEUM OF MODERN ART)

physical suffering; the ugliness of the caricature is unredeemed by adventitious grace.

This story is one of the more ambitious that Hitchcock has ever treated [1957]. There is no trace here of the thriller, the melodrama. The plot is completely dependent on the truth of the characters, and these are far from being conventional, as might initially have been believed. All that had to be done was elevate the discussion from the level of the psychology of mores to that of morality, a morality whose glaucous depths are not easily sounded. Our only reservation stems from the fact that the discussion retains an overly literary aspect, that it places insufficient faith in the innate power of cinema . . .

As might be expected, this was one of those films that found grace in the eyes of Hitchcock's usual detractors. Let us join our praise to theirs; and, secure in our sympathy for Hitch, let us say that though this is not one of his most finished works, it illuminates the others in a way that helps us understand them better. Though some of our director's films are technical experiments, this one is evidently a moral experiment, a uniquely moral experiment. The auteur here explicitly exposes a philosophy that is implicit elsewhere: his refusal to judge, his exigence, his pessimism, his legitimate suspicion of pity, justice, and other fine sentiments. What does he offer us at the end of this exercise in undermining? Merely a "middle ground," an unstable equilibrium; not ultimate wisdom but a simple emergency solution. In this life on which we are "embarked," there is only a provisional—a lifesaving—Good. A morality cynical in its conclusions though Jansenist[1] in its premises. A hypocritical morality, agreed, but a clear-sighted one. We profit from evil: let us at least know that it *is* evil from which we profit. Or—what comes to the same thing—let us expel evil, but at the same time acknowledge that its expulsion does not leave us with clean hands. Is this his final word? Hitchcock will return to the charge. We have only to wait.

At the beginning of 1944, Hitchcock obtained Selznick's permission to return to Great Britain in order to make two short propaganda films commissioned by the Ministry of Information.

The first was *Aventure Malgache*, acted in French by the Molière Players—performers who had sought refuge in England. The film told how a young lawyer had organized the Resistance in Madagas-

[1]The former student of the Jesuits often seems like an unconscious Jansenist who doesn't even know the meaning of the term: "What Is Jansenist?" (cf. interview by André Bazin. *Cahiers du Cinéma*, No. 39.

Spellbound (1945) featured Ingrid Bergman and Gregory Peck in a Freudian tale in which a psychoanalyst helps her patient regain the unity of his being. (PHOTO COURTESY OF MUSEUM OF MODERN ART)

car. It was Hitchcock's *hommage* to France, the land of good food.

The second film, *Bon Voyage,* though a much more Hitchcockian subject, was based on a true occurrence. An English prisoner of war escapes from Germany. He is accompanied by a Polish officer who has also escaped. The two men become friends, but the Englishman discovers that his companion is actually a Gestapo agent, and he kills him.

One of the scenario writers of *Bon Voyage*—Angus McPhail, a man captivated by demonology—drew Hitchcock's attention to a "detective" novel by Francis Beeding, *The House of Dr. Edwardes.* The two men worked on an adaptation, which on his return to the United States Hitch submitted to Selznick. The latter immediately raised strong objections. The film was to take place entirely in a psychiatric hospital and be done half in black and white and half in color,[1] depending upon whether sane people or madmen were concerned. The director of the hospital was also to be a madman—a high priest of black masses, who had the cross of Christ tattooed on the soles of his feet so that he could tread it underfoot with his every step.

The House of Dr. Edwardes was eventually filmed under the title *Spellbound* (1945), but this *Spellbound* no longer had any relation to Francis Beeding's novel.

Faced with Selznick's veto, Hitchcock had changed his mind and decided to construct his scenario around an actress he found particularly fascinating: Ingrid Bergman. However, as he got to know his future star, he conceived the vaster project of giving her the central role in a series of works that would throw light on the many facets of feminine personality. Thus was born the trilogy consisting of *Spellbound, Notorious,* and *Under Capricorn.*

The scenario, for which Hitchcock had obtained the collaboration of Ben Hecht, was designed to show the protective and maternal role of woman considered as guardian angel. The plot is certainly a model of logic, but its didactic nature is too obvious. The heroine, Constance, is a doctor in a psychiatric hospital. She is a woman who wears glasses, is ruled by reason, and is cold and

[1]This no doubt accounts for the red flash in *Spellbound.*

logical. The director of the institution, Dr. Murchison, is forced into retirement, and his successor, Dr. Edwardes (Gregory Peck), is being awaited. As soon as the young and handsome doctor arrives, Constance becomes troubled for the first time in her life. But she quickly realizes that the man she loves is mentally ill: he is suffering from amnesia and believes he has killed the true Dr. Edwardes. The doctor flees. Constance goes after him and installs him in the home of one of her former teachers, who, by analyzing a dream of the unfortunate man—he has in the interval become a potentially dangerous madman—discovers that he was skiing in the company of the true Dr. Edwardes when the latter fell into a chasm. To provoke a catharsis by a similarity of situation, Constance takes the amnesiac on a skiing trip. He recovers his memory and brings to the surface a guilt complex resulting from a terrible accident to his young brother, who was impaled on a spiked fence while they were playing as children. The death of Dr. Edwardes, which happened under similar circumstances (by sliding down a slope) had unseated his reason. The ending belongs to the detective story genre: Constance unmasks the true guilty party, who is none other than the former director of the psychiatric hospital.

Hitchcock does not use the portrayal of a sick man's obsessions simply as a pretext for composing some terrifying images. What interests him is the very principle of psychoanalysis. He sees in it the medical equivalent of that "confession" which is to furnish the theme of *Under Capricorn* and *I Confess*. In addition, it is the Woman who plays the role of confessor and savior. This is a far cry from the legendary misogyny of which our auteur is accused. On contact with a woman, the sick man regains his mental integrity, or more exactly, the unity of his being. On contact with the man she loves, the cold Constance, the lady doctor in spectacles, becomes completely feminine. *Spellbound* is a great film about love.

In recounting the exegesis of a symbol, it was natural to base the construction of this film on a symbol. Parallel lines and the color white obsess us, just as they obsess the sick man. The ski descent, which recalls the moment in the dream in which the amnesiac is perched on a roof, contains a more subtle allegory. It is the illustration of a theme dear to Hitchcock and which might be formulated as follows: "It is necessary to descend twice, to follow the path a second time." In *To Catch a Thief,* we will once more come across the image of a man perched on a roof, an image accompanied by the same musical theme.

The principal fault of *Spellbound* is its aridity, an aridity which may well be due to the nature of its framework, psychoanalysis. To this should be added the "negative contribution" of producer Selznick: the collaboration of Salvador Dali in the dream images was one of his ideas, and probably not the worst! Selznick is a strong personality: he wants to be "boss" on the sets where his films are produced, and he most certainly added his pinch of salt to the creation of *Spellbound.* Hitchcock freely admits that he ceded to him on many points, but he is unwilling to say which.

Notorious (1946), however, is Hitchcock's independent production for RKO. Once again Ben Hecht did the adaptation, this time based on a story suggested to the director by Marthe Richard's memoirs; but the film is only vaguely related to the adventures of the spy who sacrificed her virtue on the altar of her country!

When this admirable film, one of its auteur's most beautiful, was released in France, several critics found the subject either banal or nauseating. But the very way in which they summarized the plot showed that they hadn't understood the film.

Here is the story as Hitchcock tells it. On April 24, 1946, at 3:20 P.M., Huberman, a Nazi spy, is sentenced by an American tribunal. His daughter, Alicia, continues to live the debauched life of a high-class tart. When a government agent, Devlin (Cary Grant), suggests that she rehabilitate her name by working for the United States, she accepts. They leave for Rio. Devlin makes love to her; she falls in love with him and tries in vain to make him understand that she has changed. He loves her, too, but does not want to be forced to despise her. When he informs Alicia of the mission assigned her—to captivate her father's old friend, Alexander Sebastian, and gain entrance to his house, a veritable nest of Nazi spies—he secretly hopes that she will refuse. But Alicia, waiting for Devlin to keep her from accepting this odious assignment, does nothing of the kind. She therefore arranges to meet Sebastian, who is as taken with her as had been predicted, and who somewhat less expectedly asks her to marry him. To the great astonishment of her employers, Alicia accepts, again hoping that Devlin will object, but he persists in remaining silent, waiting for her to refuse on her own. There she is, then, in a key spot; but despite the fact that she is mistress of the house, she has great difficulty in laying her hands on a certain key, the one to the wine cellar in which Devlin, invited to a reception, will discover a bottle filled with uranium ore. But Sebastian notices that the key has been taken and that his cellar has been tampered with. Following his mother's advice, he decides to slowly poison the woman he was careless enough to marry. On reseeing Alicia, Devlin initially mistakes the effects of the poison for those of alcohol; he is nevertheless surprised when Alicia fails to keep their rendezvous, and he decides to go to her even at the risk of endangering his mission. At the house he finds the young woman prostrate in her room; he confesses his love, and threatening her husband with a revelation that would expose him to the vengeance of his accomplices, he helps Alicia leave the house. The pretense that Alicia is being taken to a hospital will not save Sebastian, and as the couple gets into the car, the door closes on him ominously.

Far from being a "repugnant story of a police prostitute," as someone blithely dubbed it, *Notorious* is the magnificent story of a woman redeemed by love. But first a word about the political viewpoint. The action is very precisely situated in time: it begins April 24, 1946, at 3:20 P.M. It is at that moment that a Nazi spy tells his judges that they will not be able to prevent the total destruction that threatens their country, that next time the Nazis will succeed. A little later we are shown, busily occupied, a professor, an "important cog in the German war machine." Once more Hitchcock identifies Nazism with a diabolical plot. Nevertheless, he does not fall into elementary Manicheanism: these diabolical creatures are also victims, and, most often, as pitiful as they are dangerous. Sebastian (Claude Rains) reminds us of Fisher, Bruno Anthony, and other demons in the Hitchcockian mythology; his mother reminds us of the housekeeper Milly in *Under Capricorn*.

As for Alicia, she is a character who is simultaneously just like and just the opposite of Constance in *Spellbound*. She is a lost woman for whom love is only a game, who keeps "a list" of her "playmates," and who cannot prevent herself from making amorous conquests. But she is also a woman who dreams of forgetting the past, of beginning a new life. When she falls in love with Devlin, her face, which Hitchcock has previously shown us as sad and vacant, lights up; this woman rediscovers her soul, and it transfigures her. It is at this point that a cruel game begins. Devlin is a "cop," and as such he has principles: a drunk doesn't change and a lost woman doesn't change. Their relationship is therefore based on a misunderstanding. But there is much more here than the classic "lovers' quarrel." The misfortune of the two protagonists comes from the fact that as victims of their mutual preconceptions, they refuse to pronounce the saving "word." They fail to appreciate the virtue of this confession, which is the key to all Hitchcock's films and which is at the heart of *Under Capricorn*.

The atmosphere of extreme sensuality that reigns in *Notorious* does not in any way clash with the abstraction of the style. In this film of close-ups, "matter"—admirably emphasized by Ted Tetzlaff's lighting (faces, metal, glass, jewels, rugs, floor tiles)—shines with a light that is alternately glacial or burning. In this plot woven of reticences and lies, only actions count; but at the same time, the latter are a facade. There are two love scenes. The first, on the terrace, is only skin-deep. It is translated by a succession of oral contacts between two people glued to each other and to whom our eyes are glued. This thirst for kisses, which seems unquenchable, expresses the vanity of the flesh when love is absent. In the second scene the fleshly contact couldn't be more simple, but the feeling is real. When Devlin, come to save Alicia from death, steps from the shadows—in the same way he had appeared after the Miami drinking bout—and the camera, in a movement of extreme tenderness and sensuality, circles around the two lovers, the screen sparkles with an indescribable beauty, the secret of which Hitchcock learned from Murnau. Even the moments when the two protagonists are in the presence of a third party smolder with a

Cary Grant and Ingrid Bergman starred in *Notorious* (1946), which many critics, especially in France, failed to appreciate as "the magnificent story of a woman redeemed by love." (PHOTO COURTESY OF THE MUSEUM OF MODERN ART)

hidden flame: when Devlin is surprised by the master of the house, he pretends to clasp Alicia in a falsely false embrace, but their feigned kiss is a real one.

However, it is not at all surprising that *Notorious* was so coldly received. Because of its deliberate mixture of the extremely concrete and the abstract, it is one of Hitchcock's most difficult works. Though the director thoroughly kneaded the malleable and richly resourceful dough of his interpreters (this is perhaps Bergman's best performance), the scenario and the shooting script, on the other hand, have the simplicity of a theorem. For the law of strict verisimilitude is substituted the logic not so much of figures as of objects (glasses of alcohol, cups of poison, and of course the key, which evokes the one in *Dial M for Murder*) by means of which the narrator tells us his story. The track shot that begins at the top of the stairway and finishes on the key in Alicia's hand is justly famous. One is reminded—such is the tendency toward "synthesis"—of certain "Kammerspiel" films. If Hitchcock evokes Murnau, the admirably constructed scenario by Ben Hecht recalls those of Carl Mayer.

Made cautious by the lukewarm critical reception of *Notorious,* and eager to put an end to the contract that bound him to Selznick, Hitch postponed some more ambitious projects (among them the third panel of the Ingrid Bergman triptych, a modern version of *Hamlet*) and agreed to film Robert Hichens's novel *The Paradine Case.* Initially, he intended to treat it as a sort of Lady Chatterley thriller. But Selznick, whose name was on the scenario, didn't see it this way: it was he who chose the actors and insisted on Louis Jourdan for the groom, whereas the director would have preferred a "clod." For the role of the judge, however, Hitchcock obtained his old confederate Charles Laughton. In short, after compromise had followed compromise, *The Paradine Case* was released in 1947. It resembled *Rebecca* to the extent that a producer's films resemble one another. Fortunately, as was true with *Rebecca,* Hitchcock did more than simply carry out instructions.

As the title indicates, the film relates the trial of the beautiful

In *The Paradine Case* (1947), a lawyer (Gregory Peck) defending a woman charged with murdering her husband falls in love with his client and becomes convinced of her innocence. (PHOTO COURTESY OF THE MUSEUM OF MODERN ART)

Mrs. Paradine, who is accused of having murdered her blind husband. A young lawyer, Keane (Gregory Peck), is charged with her defense. Though married to a charming young woman, he falls madly in love with Mrs. Paradine, who convinces him of her innocence. But on being invited to the Paradine estate, Keane discovers that the groom, André Latour, had been his client's lover. When the trial begins, Keane finds himself confronted with Judge Horfield, who hates the lawyer because he, the judge, had been rejected by Mrs. Keane. The intense struggle begins, and little by little the defense collapses. Latour's suicide is its *coup de grâce:* Mrs. Paradine admits her crime and publicly reveals that Keane is in love with her. The lawyer's career is destroyed, as is his great love. He will try to find forgetfulness in the arms of his wife.

Of the three themes in this story that interested Hitchcock, only one—Mrs. Paradine's wild, animal love for Latour—failed to come across on the screen, and this because of improper casting. The other two, however, are admirably brought out. The judge, a fat and revolting libertine with a lubricious eye and unctuous behavior, occupies an important place in the gallery of Hitchcockian monsters. Laughton is never better than when directed by Hitchcock: he is something to see as he plays cat and mouse with the unfortunate Keane. When the lawyer leans toward his client, the judge showers him with ribald glances—forcing him to tighten the bonds of complicity that unite him to Mrs. Paradine—and then suddenly drops his mask, narrows his eyes like a jackal as he poses insidious questions, and then bursts into laughter. Hitch has a sharp sense of caricature; his fading women, his model employees, his cops, his homosexuals, are justly famous creations. The judge he gives us here is enough to shake our faith in the English magistracy.

Finally, we once more come across that "temptation of the fall" which was the subject of *Downhill, The Manxman,* and *Notorious.* The more base Mrs. Paradine's secret is shown to be, the more inflamed is Keane's desire. The apple in the Hitchcockian garden draws the lawyer irresistibly. He goes through every phase— including jealousy, including self-disgust. Even at the moment of her confession, if Mrs. Paradine were to open her arms to him, he would rapturously throw himself into them. But the world of abasement, like the world of espionage, is a closed one. The terrible and magnificent feeling (not once is the word "love" spoken) that unites these two people carries its own punishment within it. Only public *confession* can wash Keane's shame away. The camera, in a high-angle shot, slowly approaches his face as he pleads for himself, and it comes to a halt with a close-up that shows a face as weary as death. The lens immediately reassumes the position of God; like a drunken fly, Keane weaves his way out of the court, diagonally traversing the screen from right to left, from bottom to top.

Thus, despite the inevitable traces of academicism inherent in an over-controlled production, the Selznick period closed at a high point. Is it coincidence that *The Paradine Case,* by its form, in some way evokes *Rebecca?* Hitchcock has a sense of symmetry. All that matters is that between the first and last film for Selznick the director of *The Lady Vanishes* has become the director of *Notorious.* He has polished up his arms, made himself a universe. It is now sufficiently familiar to allow us—without abandoning chronological order—to expose the great themes of his work and the general characteristics of his style, which until now we have only alluded to.

THE AMERICAN PERIOD (2): ROPE TO THE MAN WHO KNEW TOO MUCH (1948-1956)

The Conquest of Continuity
Rope (1948)

The Paradine Case marked the end of the Selznick-Hitchcock association. The film-maker, who for all practical purposes had seen to the production of *Suspicion* and *Notorious* himself, decided to create an independent company. He joined with Sidney Bernstein, the owner of a large chain of movie theaters in Great Britain, and founded Transatlantic Pictures.

Hitchcock was at last free to undertake the making of that *Under Capricorn* so dear to his heart. But fearing a commercial failure, he preferred first to shoot a film that would be relatively inexpensive, look revolutionary, and serve as a kind of technical rough draft.

Long takes had been in fashion for several years. *Rope,* carrying this tendency further, was to consist of a single shot. To maintain the sense of continuity in both time and space, the interruptions due to the insertion of new film rolls in the camera were camouflaged. Half the time this was done by ending one roll and beginning the next with a close-up of the back of someone's jacket. The rest of the time it was done by picking up on glances, by cheating on the letter if not completely on the spirit, since it is these latter splices that are least perceptible.[1]

Even if nothing more than a technical challenge was involved, we have to admit that it was won hands down. As for Hitchcock, he has never mentioned anything but the practical advantage of the undertaking. The TMT (ten-minute take)—it requires about ten minutes to project a 300-meter camera roll—cuts down on actual shooting time and consequently on overall costs. The making of *Rope* took only 13 days.* The work plan established was extremely precise. Two sets were built, one for rehearsals, the other for actual filming. A system of light signals alerted the actors and the technical crew to the exact movements they would have to make.

Needless to say, the TMT is not as easy as it looks. Hitch needed every bit of his experience to bring off, in a relaxed manner, effects that many of his colleagues would have sweated over in vain: for example, the kitchen door that swings just long enough to let us see John Dall set down the rope used in the murder, or those struggling hands reframed in a close-up without sacrificing any of the scuffle's naturalness.

Though technique seems to be the most important element in this film, the script created from Patrick Hamilton's play is actually one of the most Hitchcockian. Two young men strangle a friend and hide his body in a chest. What do they have against the victim? They deny his right to live, to be weak, to marry an insignificant girl—or, reading between the lines, to love a woman. Let us not allow ourselves to be too fascinated by this latter key. Like that of misogyny, it may well close more doors than it opens. Suffice it to say that Hitchcock's characters are not unaware of the thousand

[1]There was no other way. Hitchcock took into account the fact that projection reels are double (600 meters) the length of camera rolls. To pick up on the "black" of jackets would have required from the projectionists a precision that could not be regularly counted on in practice. For this reason, every 600 meters—approximately, since the length of shot-sequences is unequal—we have a classic reverse shot.

*Translator's note: In François Truffaut's *Hitchcock* (1967), the auteur gives shooting time as 18 days.

and one faces of vice, and that homosexuality, which has played a real part in *Murder!* and which will be implied in *Strangers on a Train*, is one of them.

The body is placed in a chest a few minutes before the dead man's parents and fiancée are expected to arrive for a cocktail party. And it is at this point that Brandon (John Dall), the instigator of the crime, is overcome by the vertigo that Edgar Allan Poe has called the "imp of the perverse." He plays with fire by expounding, as the others look on half-scandalized and half-amused, the very theory that led him to murder: the superman has all rights, including that of eliminating the imbecile foolhardy enough to get in his way. This theory had been inspired in him by one of his former professors (James Stewart), who has also been invited to the "agape."

As can be seen from this outline, Hitchcock's usual leitmotifs are present. The attractive criminal, morally blackmailing his mentor, dazzles the gallery with the same sophism used by Uncle Charlie in *Shadow of a Doubt;* the terrified accomplice is the lamentable brother of the Joan Fontaines and Ingrid Bergmans of yore. Suspense is created in two ways: by showing real events and by portraying character. Brandon pushes his bluff—self-indulgence, but also supreme calculation—until it turns against him. Once suspicion is aroused, the solution to the problem of detection is demonstrated only in esthetic terms—or, if one prefers, elegantly. The ending, however, in which we see the defeated faces of the two murderers and their professor, will for a few moments restore a moral illumination to the drama.

The lines of force between the protagonists can be woven into a more complex web, as we have seen in previous films and will see again in those to come. The blackmail is only lightly sketched in; the theme of the transfer of guilt will find a more eloquent and a more purely cinematic expression in *Under Capricorn*. True, this film is one of our director's more "formal" works, but that doesn't mean that the purpose of form is only to sustain dramatic interest or to handle a paradoxical situation with maximum ease.

During these years, Hitchcock showed a fondness for extraordinary situations and unusual characters, but he nevertheless

James Stewart and Farley Granger struggle for possession of a pistol in *Rope* (1948), a tale in which a professor's disciples take too literally his theories on the rights of supermen.

insisted on illuminating the most ordinary circumstances of the drama. The important element in *Rope* is neither the corpse in the chest nor the commonplace cocktail party given by two young New York snobs; it is rather the simultaneous presence of these two orders of facts, the thorough amalgamation of two stylistic genres, the realistic and the thriller. Over the two previously pointed out kinds of "suspense" is superimposed a third line of current which is the very opposite of a suspense: the deliberate use of continuity in time and space—the famous formal postulate that slips through the back door and into the heart of the matter, in this case the film's affective and moral climate.

If the talent of the maker of *Rope* were confined to laying bare the muscles and nerves of the plot, we might be right in considering him nothing more than a fine craftsman. But he is always able to clad this somewhat spare anatomy with the splendor of a flesh known as *poetry*. This splendor, this poetry, are part of the time in which the drama is taking place, and he in no way neglects their powers. Thanks to a skillful system of lighting, thanks above all to the use of color, we pass imperceptibly from the sunny afternoon of the murder to the night of the last few minutes. It is impossible to forget either the dying man's cry, muffled in the shadows of the closed curtains, or, at the very end, when James Stewart goes to open the window, the mass of fresh air that seems to rise from the dark street. Perhaps for the first time in cinematic history, a director tried to relate color to emotional states without departing from the strictest realism.

What an extraordinary moment is that in which Farley Granger, in order to calm his nerves, starts playing Francis Poulenc's "Perpetual Movement No. 1" on the piano! Daylight is slowly fading, the guests have gone into the other room to look at some books; the hubbub of their conversation mingles with the music. This is more than a pause in the course of the drama; it is a peace heavy with a double anguish: the anguish proper to the actual situation of Granger digesting his defeat and Stewart his suspicion, but also the anguish which is part of the hour itself and which harmoniously blends with the first kind. Like a sustained bass, the pulse of real time rhythmically joins with that of the action, which is alternately slowed down and speeded up. Suddenly the professor goes to the piano and turns on the lamp, the yellow nimbus of which makes the twilight take on a bluish cast . . . The intermission is over; a new act begins without the curtain having been lowered, without the slightest disruption in life or the flow of time.

This is a grace granted only to the greatest: Hitchcock possesses the precious art of being able to linger over his model with the unhurried and meticulous eye of a painter without in any way slowing up the time of his narrative. He magically manages to transmute into supple flesh what was originally seen as the spare and arbitrary framework of one of his most deliberate works.

Hostile to the abstract hypothesis, most American and European critics were also blind to the concrete demonstration. For every Claude Mauriac who pointed out the great "importance" of *Rope*, there was a chorus of those who felt that their beloved theories or lazy habits were threatened.

There is no point in lingering over these critics whose ridiculousness has been exposed by time. The only serious objection was formulated by André Bazin. He felt that Hitchcock's film only seemed revolutionary. Why deny oneself any break in the shot only to reconstitute the classic shot breakdown? "This mise-en-scène by means of a continuous track shot that is only a perpetual succession of reframings is very different from the deep-focus shot used by Welles and Wyler, which managed to integrate several moments of a virtual montage in a single frame."

If Hitchcock's goal had been to propose a language that was a break with conventional cinematic language, Bazin would undoubtedly be right. However, Hitchcock is expressing himself in the same manner he had previously used, and would continue to use in the future.[1] At the very most he replaces coordination by subordination. But in point of fact, does the originality of Welles

---

[1] Hitchcock's style is narrative. His camera chooses, relates, takes sides. Nevertheless, after *Rope*, the arbitrary—for the arbitrary is inevitable—is disguised under the appearances of objectivity. In this sense it can be said that *Notorious*, with its explanatory camera movements, its "subjective" shots, closes a phase.

and Wyler really lie in calling the "classic shot breakdown" into question? What we object to in the latter is not that it alternates between "field" and "reverse field," but that it abolishes the *feeling* of a continuous space. The visual freedom enjoyed by the spectator of a deep-focus shot in *Citizen Kane* is completely theoretical, since only the front or the back of the field will hold our attention, depending on whether the dramatic interest puts the accent on the one or the other. If it can be said that the mise-en-scène of *Rope* is only a camouflaged classic shot breakdown, then it is even more clear that Welles's deep focus, like Gance's polyvision, is a montage spread over a surface. Virtual or real, as to expression, it amounts to the same thing. It is not this on which the novelty depends. And besides, *Othello* and *Mr. Arkadin,* the most discontinuous movies we have seen since the passing of silent films, were to give the game away.

The real conquest of modern cinema is therefore not the challenging of the "classic shot breakdown" but that of the *frame*—that Eisensteinian frame to which Orson Welles remains archaically faithful. In cinemascope films, for example, the extreme ends of the screen are for all practical purposes useless. The point is not that the frame contains more but that what is contained seems less oppressive. When employed with skill, the frame is, to use Bazin's expression, a veritable "keyhole"—but an ideal, a mobile, keyhole, the infinitely malleable contours of which are not noticeable. The spectator's visual freedom is only theoretical: he is less aware of the limits imposed on him and feels he can freely promenade through the decor, which he is more familiar with since it is shown in greater detail. Cinemascope hasn't resulted in a new esthetic: it has brought to the contemporary scene a style which had previously been the exclusive attribute of a few great precursors—Renoir, Rossellini, Hitchcock. None of the three has personally made use of it. This may be due to circumstances—but it is also true that they never felt the need. They had already gone beyond it.

Rope is an example rather than a model—an example that was followed despite what was said of it, despite its auteur's return to a discontinuous style. It contributed in no small way to freeing the film-maker from his obsession with painting and making of him what he had been in the time of Griffith and the pioneers—an *architect*. It put the set back into a position of honor and revived the importance of the actor's *performance*. It is this very confidence in the dramatic interpreter, the more precise and more continuous effort demanded of him, that seems to be the distinguishing mark of contemporary cinema. Writing in 1938, Hitchcock had argued against the long takes he was to champion ten years later. These about-faces could be held against him if he were content merely to follow fashion, but the fact is that most often he created fashion. What was truth before 1940 was an error afterward. If he is mistaken, all cinema joins him in this error.

The Secret and the Confession
Under Capricorn (1949)

The considerable commercial success of *Rope* allowed Hitchcock to prepare, in the way he wanted, for the production of *Under Capricorn*, which he filmed in Great Britain. His great dream was coming true.

The filming was a veritable nightmare. Ingrid Bergman's mind was on other things and relations between the director and his leading lady were therefore somewhat clouded. Add to this the film's resounding commercial failure, and we can understand why the memory of a work into which he put so much of himself is so painful to Hitchcock.

Nevertheless, the "unknown masterpiece," as Jean Domarchi calls it, is without doubt the best story he ever treated. In other words, "on paper" it had a literary quality generally lacking in the scenarios of his other films.

Curiously disliked by most critics, who taxed it with being a melodrama even though the plot, free of theatricalism and improbabilities, rests entirely on the drive of the passions, the film was brilliantly rehabilitated by two articles, one by Jacques Rivette in *La Gazette du Cinéma*, No. 4, and the other by Jean Domarchi in *Cahiers du Cinéma*, No. 39. We can do no better than repeat the heart of their commentary. "Hitchcock," Domarchi tells us, "was admired for the wrong reason, for suspense . . . How then could we be anything but disconcerted by a film that with amazing ease takes up the fundamental leitmotif of world literature?" This leitmotif is to be found in nineteenth-century English novels, in Balzac (*Honorine, The Village Curé*), and in Goethe (*Elective Affinities*). The theme common to all these works is not only the eternal conflict between liberty and morality (generally resolved by renunciation in favor of the latter), but the burden of a remorse or a scruple from which the hero—and more often yet the heroine—is freed only by a confession. "The secret subject of this drama," wrote Jacques Rivette, "is *confession*, the liberation from a secret, liberation in its double meaning: in the pyschoanalytical sense, because it frees us from memory by giving memory a verbal form, and in the religious sense; in this case the confession of sins is the same as their redemption."

This is indeed the subject of *I Confess*, but also that of Rossellini's *La Paura*, or the episode of the medallion in Bresson's *Diary of a Country Priest*. Hitchcock embroiders the motif with a second idea: that of disintegration, of a taint which contaminates the soul and then the body. This concept of a close affinity between the flesh and the spirit, a concept on which all western art is based, is much despised by our moderns: but suddenly the cinema, by simply presenting the evidence, furnishes it with a contemporary and irrefutable foundation.

Australia in 1835. Charles Adare (Michael Wilding), nephew of the governor, newly arrived from England, is invited to dine at the home of Sam Flusky (Joseph Cotten), who is married to one of his cousins. The latter, Lady Henrietta (Ingrid Bergman), is sunk in a stupor due in part to alcohol, a stupor skillfully maintained by Milly, the housekeeper. Charles decides to cure Henrietta, to free her from this influence, and little by little he falls in love with her. Sam's jealousy, reinforced by Milly's insinuations, erupts during a public ball. Scandal. After the ball, Henrietta discloses the truth to Charles. It is she who has committed the murder for which her husband had accepted the responsibility. She killed her brother, who reproached her for allowing herself to be courted by a commoner. A new quarrel erupts between Sam and Charles, during the course of which the latter is wounded. To save the former convict from the sentence that threatens him, Charles and Henrietta give up their nascent love. "The transfer of the responsibility for sin had in the past divided the couple, one assuming the punishment, the other the guilt; this inadequately accepted sacrifice forces them to give themselves up to the intoxication of other mutual sacrifices, incessantly renewed; and it will only be possible for them to renounce sacrifice and accept happiness if a third person assumes this sacrifice in his turn" (J.R.). The moral exigency of the protagonists is then extreme. "Hitchcock," Domarchi observes, "here as always deliberately opts for heaven and against hell; but unlike what he does in his other films, he here grants heaven a great deal of space . . . *Under Capricorn* is the exact converse of his 'films noirs.' The basic theme of the 'secret' that binds one conscience to another is the point of departure for an undertaking not of enslavement but of liberation."

In spite of the film's high moral tone, Hitchcock uses the most violent means of playing on our nerves. Is this a concession? A happy concession, since it provides us with one of the most significant close-ups in the entire history of cinema. We are in the last quarter hour of the film. Milly knows that her mistress's physical resistance has reached its limits and that a sudden shock will be enough to kill her. She therefore hides under the bedcover one of those mummified human heads made by the natives. Henrietta finds it, utters a muffled cry, and sinks to the foot of the bed, half unconscious. Milly, believing that she has fainted, replaces the head in its basket. A very large close-up then shows us Henrietta slowly opening her eyes, and her face immediately expresses such a wealth of different feelings (fear and self-control, candor and calculation, rage and resignation) that the most concise pen would require several pages to express it all. In fact, these few seconds are no less extraordinary than those pages in Dostoyevsky's *The Little One* in which his protagonist, having instinctively opened his eyes at the moment when his wife is holding a revolver to his temple, wonders if she knows that he has seen her or merely

attributes the flutter of his eyelids to a normal gesture of sleep. The novelist and the film-maker were both able—the one through verbal description and the other through the genius proper to *his* art—to derive the richest and most subtle meaning from a situation that is no less melodramatic in the first case than in the second. This is not the first time that we can find a resemblance between Hitchcock's work and that of Dostoyevsky. *Rope* is closer in spirit

to *Crime and Punishment* than all the cinematic adaptations that have been made of that novel. This short scene is even more striking: the analogy is not only in the situation but in the treatment, in the detail, the beauty of which is completely dependent on the direction.

In this film Hitchcock continues his experiments with the long take. But he appreciably relaxes the rigor of the rule: only one shot, that of Henrietta's confession, lasts the length of a whole film roll. Neither the unity of place (we rarely leave Sam's house, but we do nevertheless leave), nor that of time (the structure is novelistic and no longer that of drama) is respected. The camera moves with an extreme ease and audacity (the "fourth side," made to vanish in *Rope,* is often shown us), but the decor is considerably less important to the action than previously. Though we shall not, as Rivette does, speak of "a certain plastic ugliness that throws the completely moral beauty of the work into relief," we confess that this period film is one of its auteur's most abstract, and that the color, though often beautiful, rarely contributes to the meaning. The role of objects is also reduced to a minimum.

On the other hand, the camera hugs the characters more and more closely. This film, as was already true in *Notorious,* is the story of a face, that of Ingrid Bergman. It is this face that the lens scrutinizes, searches, now etching it, now softening it. It is to this face that the homage of the most beautiful effects is made. Among others, the one pointed out by François Truffaut: when Charles holds his jacket behind a pane of glass and forces Henrietta, who had done away with all mirrors lest she find her disintegration reflected in them, to contemplate her still untouched beauty. The performances, though more lyrical, are nevertheless free of all theatrical emphasis. Our attention is concentrated on the actors, who do not, however, indulge in any brilliant "bits" on their own responsibility. The mechanical precision of the direction is tyrannical only where the actors are concerned, but the behavior of the characters they portray, liberated from the conventions of ordinary cinematic language, reveals itself freely.

In *Rebecca,* Laurence Olivier delivers a long monologue that prefigures Ingrid Bergman's: here the camera never leaves the actress, whereas in the earlier film a descriptive track shot of the set introduces a diversion. True, the confession is a bravura piece, but let's not be dazzled by technical prowess. And especially let's not see in this long speech merely an artifice designed to reveal to the spectator events that took place prior to the beginning of the film. The monologue or confidence, common theatrical methods, is here an *end,* a privileged and even an extraordinary moment.

We do not go from speech to speech but from silence to speech, from reticence to *confession*. The fact that the heroine finally speaks is as important as what she tells us: "Words serve as a 'catharsis,' they mark the triumph of truth over appearances"(J. D.).

The majestic beauty of *Under Capricorn* foreshadows that of *I Confess*. These films are related not only by theme but by rhythm, both having been conceived like a slow but sure march punctuated by abrupt halts. Though neither one scorns to jangle our nerves, the very baldness of these effects purifies them, makes them more "fascinating" than really terrifying. At the highest point of the emotion in which they grip us they nevertheless permit us the distance necessary to the contemplation of great works of art. This distance need only be taken once. The profundity of this work having been brought out, it will somehow reflect light onto the other films.

Virtuosity
Stage Fright (1950)

It is difficult to imagine the direction Alfred Hitchcock would have taken if *Under Capricorn* had achieved the results he had banked on. He would most likely have continued along this austere and dangerous path. As it happened, failure once more drove him to take a deliberate step back. He agreed to film in England, for Robert Clark of Associated British, a detective thriller adapted from Selwyn Jepson's *Man Running*. This was *Stage Fright*.

Needless to say, he had been given a completely free hand. He shaped the scenario so as to bring out the two elements that interested him: on the one hand, the portrait of a young woman, an apprentice actress who will be given her first role by the circumstances of real life; on the other, a technical innovation—a cinematic lie to which we will return later.

The story is very ordinary. A young woman, Eve (Jane Wyman), receives the confidences of her childhood friend, Jonathan (Richard Todd), who is sought by the police for the murder of the husband of his mistress, Charlotte (Marlene Dietrich). Jonathan explains to Eve that Charlotte is the murderer and that he is the unfortunate victim of appearances. Eve agrees to hide him in the home of her parents, amiable eccentrics, and disguising herself, she wins entrance to Charlotte's home in order to unmask her. But Eve discovers that Jonathan has lied to her and that he really is the murderer. He tries to kill her before being crushed by the iron safety curtain of a theater. Eve will be all the more easily consoled for her error thanks to Inspector Smith (Michael Wilding), who is in charge of the investigation and smothers her with tender glances all during the second half of the film.

Stage Fright is not an ambitious work, but a very intelligent sort of superior entertainment: a series of half-comic, half-serious variations on a theme which is itself only a pretext. The film can be thought of as the promenade of a director who is particularly attentive to the gentle poetry of gracious gestures, to the freshness of a young girl's soul, to the charm of certain privileged moments. But he is also sensitive to disquieting detail, to the fascination of voluptuousness, to sheathed violence, to powdered and polished Evil.

We are given a gallery of portraits that are simultaneously delicate and savage, lucid and amused; a succession of delicious or strangely morbid scenes. It is difficult to isolate the dominant theme. The film is a succession of scenes rather than a work. And perhaps that makes it easier for us to appreciate better the refinement of Hitchcockian art. For example, we understand what makes the first meeting between Eve (disguised) and Charlotte so striking: that slight forward track toward the woman in widow's weeds, that finger sensually gliding between the breasts, that simultaneously strange, guttural, and soft voice of the actress (played by Marlene Dietrich). We are made uneasy by this shot, as though suddenly aware of an evil spell.

It is by studying a film like *Stage Fright* shot by shot that one may be able to grasp the secrets of Hitchcock's form. Because it is less unified, less perfect, than the great films of our cineast, it dazzles us more. The most beautiful scene takes place in a taxi. It is hardly more than a succession of shots and reverse shots but Hitchcock has found the way to go beyond the words and make us understand what these people think, to render fascinating this exchange of thoughts that search each other out, meet, or flee. When Eve and Inspector Smith get into the cab, she is a young girl and he a detective. They talk of this and that. When the taxi pulls up, it is a couple of lovers who get out, without either one of them having made the least gesture toward the other. This is more worthy of the name virtuosity than a 30-mile track shot.

Another example: Jonathan's famous lie. When, at the very beginning of the film, he gives his version of events to Eve, he gives a *cinematic* version: the images that illustrate his narrative are seen on the screen. At the end of the film, we learn that he has lied. By a logical process, the spectator thinks that the images have lied with him: indignation (this was before *Rashomon!*). But such is not the case. In Hitchcock films, the images never lie, though the characters do. The same sequence shown without the soundtrack can illustrate the true version of events. It is the commentary that makes it false, that lies, that assigns the actions *another* cause, another goal. Sleight of hand, it will be objected. Not at all. The subject of *Stage Fright,* the straight line around which the arabesques curl, is Eve, the young girl who stands for non-duplicity. Her universe does not include lies. She believes (and of course the spectator joins her in this) in Jonathan's innocence, and she plunges into the adventure blindly. The theme of this film is thus related to that of *Shadow of a Doubt,* upon which it throws a brighter light. The *revelation* of the lie is at the heart of the story. Far from being an artifice, the lying account given by Jonathan is the very basis of the film. In this light the arabesques themselves lose their apparent gratuitousness, since they are variations on the theme of innocence.

The culminating point of *Stage Fright,* that scrupulously reconstructed English benefit garden party, quickly reveals the film's riches. This is especially true of the part about the doll, in which one might see—and this in itself would be pretty good—no more than the cinematic expression of the progression of an idea. The sequence of shots is approximately as follows:

1) Alastair Sim (Eve's father) hears a song by Charlotte, whom he too suspects of the crime. He knows that at the time of the crime Charlotte's dress was stained by her husband's blood.

2) He sees a doll at a rifle stand and tries to buy it, but he has to shoot to win it.

3) He makes a small cut on his finger and stains the doll's dress with blood.

4) He spots a cub scout and gets him to take the doll to Charlotte, who is on stage.

5) The cub scout presents the doll to Charlotte, who falters in her singing.

This last shot, for which the entire sequence had been created, is effective only because of the presence of the *cub scout,* symbol of innocence. We might have chosen five or even ten other examples; every scene in this film is based on the innocence of the character involved.

A cool oasis amidst a series of stifling and austere works, *Stage Fright* also completes a cycle. The next film was to be *I Confess,* but the special nature of the story, and the freedom with which Hitchcock planned to treat it, temporarily frightened the censors. Unwilling to make any concessions, and considering this work very important, he delayed the making of it and undertook another film, one based on a novel by Patricia Highsmith.

Figure and Number
Strangers on a Train (1951)

Alfred Hitchcock's stories come from a great variety of sources, but very early on, he began to alter them in his own way, setting to work on the double job of purifying and enriching them. First he trims the basic idea to bring out a pure relation of force between the characters. Once this has been established, he draws from it, like so many consequences of this relationship, each of the events of the plot. Generally speaking, this deduction operates on two parallel levels, the physical and the moral, and establishes a relation of symbol to idea.

We have already seen this deductive and symbolic aspect in many parts of the English films. The handcuff scene in *The Thirty-Nine Steps* is a humorous expression of the idea of solidarity, one of the aspects of the "exchange." Little by little, the system was to become more coherent, and for each given work the "finds" gushed from the same vein. The films became more homogeneous, and the formulas governing their construction could be more and more easily isolated. It is these formulas that we must return to if we want to study Hitchcock's symbolism; it is these formulas that we must keep our eyes on if we venture to use the dangerous word "metaphysics." As we have often pointed out, it is in the form that we must look for the depth of the work and that form is heavy with a latent metaphysic. It is therefore important to consider Hitchcock's work in the same way we would that of an esoteric painter or poet. The fact that the key to the system is not always in the lock, that the doors themselves are skillfully camouflaged, is no reason to insist that there is nothing inside.

We must follow through to the end; it is not enough to disclose a certain fetichism of situations and objects; we must also look for the relationship that unites these same situations or objects. We must go back to the purest essences of Figure and Number.

Let us therefore give substance to the idea of *exchange* in the form of a refrain, something that comes and goes. Let us inscribe a circle over that straight line, trouble that inertia with a swirling movement. Suddenly our figure emerges, our reaction is released. There is not even one effect in *Strangers on a Train* that does not come from this matrix. The film begins with close-ups of *steps,* and these close-ups establish the rhythm and the tone. Hitchcock firmly returns to a discontinuous style: the confined space of a continuous decor cannot be allowed to contain the dominant rectilinear that must here be extended as far as possible; the void separating the two men must be felt. But nonetheless space here is not less present, tangible, full—logically, if not actually. Then we find ourselves in the train, messenger of that implied continuity.

Two men are talking in a compartment: one, Guy (Farley Granger), is a champion tennis player; the other, Bruno (Robert Walker), represents himself as one of his fans. Bruno talks of the *vertigo* of modern life, of its intoxication and *speed;* and then he makes a proposal to Guy. He first explains that what makes a crime imperfect is the fact that the motive of its author can be discovered. He then suggests that they eliminate motives by an *exchange* of crimes: he will kill Guy's wife, who refuses to divorce him, and Guy will kill Bruno's father. Guy rejects Bruno's proposal, but because he cannot persuade his wife, a saleswoman in a *record* shop, to divorce him, he will be unable to marry the woman he loves—Ann, the daughter of a senator. As for Bruno, he decides to forge ahead.

He lies in wait for Guy's wife, who goes to an amusement park with two men. There running into a child who is dressed as a cowboy and who playfully points his pistol at him, Bruno bursts the boy's *balloon* with a burning cigarette. Then the group embarks on a *lake* at the exit to the *labyrinth* of a *tunnel.* A game of hide and seek follows: Bruno seizes the opportunity to strangle (in other words to *encircle* within his hands) the *round* throat of Guy's wife. The scene is filmed in the lenses of her *glasses,* which have fallen to the ground. The murderer is then in a position to blackmail the tennis player, whom he keeps under a sort of *spell,* making him assume the responsibility for the crime from which he has profited. At every turn of the road he appears to Guy as his own image reflected in a mirror that scarcely distorts it, as Guy's evil *double.* (This phenomenon of possession once more evokes Dostoyevsky.)

But this perfect technician of crime is actually a psychopath. Strangling Guy's wife was as much a pleasure to him as an act of calculation. His hatred of his father, his attentiveness to his mother, his desire for destruction, for escape, his frenzied scheming, leave no doubt as to the Oedipal origin of his psychosis; it is the *roundness* and the *whiteness* of that throat which fascinated him. Like the teeth of Poe's Berenice, it is an idea. Bruno will rediscover that idea in the *round* throat and the *glasses* of the senator's younger daughter. It is she whom he will contemplate while pretending to play at strangling one of the women at a reception he has crashed. And through his skill in portraying transfers and substitutions of all kinds, Hitchcock masterfully makes us participate in the terror of the young girl who realizes that she is the object of the desire of which the other woman is the victim. Bruno, who has partially betrayed himself, decides to cover his tracks by placing at the scene of the crime a cigarette lighter he had taken from Guy when they first met on the train. This will give us a chase preceded by a tennis match (note once more the *exchange* and the *white ball*).

Bruno loses precious time in retrieving the lighter, which has slipped down a sewer trap, while Guy manages to escape the surveillance of the detectives thanks to the complicity of Ann's sister, who has spilled her face powder (*white*) over one of them. He will be able to catch a *train* as the *disk* of the sun sinks on the horizon and Bruno, standing near the lake, awaits his turn at getting into a boat. For several moments, natural time substitutes for artificial suspense time, just as it did throughout *Rope*. Bruno, unmasked by the ticket-taker, has no other recourse but to jump onto a whirling *merry-go-round,* which the owner unsuccessfully tries to stop. There is a savage struggle on the platform, which *turns* faster and faster while the children, thinking it a game, laugh. Hitchcock's cruelty is a new version of that in *Sabotage.* Finally the children understand; they are panic-stricken, and contrary to our expectations, their fears are borne out: the merry-go-round *bursts,* comes apart, and sinks down amidst screams and the noise of breaking beams. Bruno is dead. Guy is saved and will savor in peace the fruit of another's crime.

Those who care to are free to insist that these different motifs of the straight line, the circle, the back and forth motion, the whirling movement, the number two, and the color white[1] are to be found in this film completely by chance. But in that case the same chance

[1]This last motif is secondary, and besides it is purely contingent: white is the color of a tennis game. But Hitchcock (aided by Robert Burks, the cameraman) knew how to take advantage of the disquieting aspect of this white—milky and not bright—conceived as a positive and evil color and not as an absence, an emblem of purity.

has to be used to explain their presence in some of Edgar Allan Poe's stories. That their introduction both here and in Poe is always deliberate is not certain, nor would it even be desirable. A great creator is like a good geometrist, in whom intuition precedes and guides reasoning. He makes his construction and leaves to scholiasts the burden of working out the sterile demonstration.

But let us return to this notion of form. We were saying that it is in form that basic essence resides, just as skin, according to biologists, is the original and therefore essential part of an organism. The weak point in *Spellbound* was that the character is depicted as a clinical "case." Psychoanalysis was the prima donna of the film, and esthetics followed along as best it could. Here, on the contrary, the object that haunts Bruno is not presented to us in its strangeness, but in what it shares with the most ordinary and harmless of our tendencies. And this is done through the intermediary of form.

The attraction of murder, a taste for scheming, sexual perversion, and sick pride are taints presented under the aspects of Figure and Number, depicted in a way that is sufficiently abstract and universal for us to recognize a difference of degree rather than of kind between the obsessions of the protagonist and our own obsessions. Bruno's criminal attitude is only a debased form of an attitude basic to all human beings. In his sickness we can distinguish—corrupted, perverted, but given a kind of esthetic dignity—the very archetype of all our desires. His crime is only that he put into execution what Guy, and we ourselves, took merely for an intellectual game, just as did the old woman who imprudently offered him her throat. By killing, he fulfills our desires as spectators, just as he fulfills the amorous desires of the tennis player. We are as much on his side as we are on Guy's. It's all a back and forth motion, a crossing over; and the screen itself, this chasm that separates reality from fiction, is not enough of a barrier to prevent our participation. Like the sister of Guy's fiancée in the strangling scene, we are spectators; and yet, like her, we find ourselves more involved than we care to admit.

Hitchcock's art, thrown into particularly sharp relief by this film, is to make us participate—by means of the fascination

Farley Granger and Robert Walker are originally only *Strangers on a Train* (1951), but their fates become involved when a mutually advantageous pact is suggested. (PHOTO COURTESY OF THE MUSEUM OF MODERN ART)

exercised over each of us by a figure that is almost geometrically refined—in the vertigo of the characters; and beyond this vertigo we discover the essence of the moral idea. The current that goes from the symbol to the idea always passes through the condenser of emotion. It is never a theoretic or a conventional connection. The emotion is a means and not an end in itself, as for example it is in the horror plays of the Grand Guignol. This emotion is on the other side of the form, but on this side of the idea. Because of this, it sometimes leaves us with both a bitter taste in our mouths and the sense of a Unity which is the Unity of the world itself.

In the midst of chaos, this Unity is always discernible and provides a source of light that plays some of its most beautiful rays over the somber facets of Evil. Nature traverses this film from end to end—the everyday nature of festive evenings and sunny afternoons, but also nature with a capital N, or more exactly *cosmos*, a world spinning amidst other spinning worlds. Each gesture, each thought, each material or moral being, is the depository of a secret capable of explaining everything: and this light dispenses as much fear as comfort. The *same* principle on which the foundation of the world is based is simultaneously the principle that can preside at its destruction. We ask ourselves, as do the protagonists of *Shadow of a Doubt* in the film's closing moments, if the world doesn't at times go mad. This idea, expressed in that film by words, is presented here in a concrete, irrefutable fashion. We are literally caught up in the maelstrom of universal gravitation. Edgar Allan Poe, the author of *Eureka,* has not been invoked in vain.

The Temptation of Martyrdom
I Confess (1952)

I Confess is the story of a priest who is a prisoner to the secret of the confessional. We have already had occasion to mention the role of Christianity in Hitchcock's work, and we will return to it later. This Christianity is not of the combative kind. As we have already noted, though Hitchcock is a practicing Catholic, he has nothing of the mystic or the ardent proselyte about him. His works are of a profane nature, and though they often deal with questions relating to God, their protagonists are not gripped by an anxiety that is properly speaking religious.

And yet there is not one of Hitchcock's films that is not more or less marked by Christian ideas and symbols. The notion of Providence runs through them like filigree work, materializing in a few scattered signs like Hannay's Bible in *The Thirty-Nine Steps* or the sudden discovery of the boat in *Rebecca*. It almost breaks through to the surface in the second version of *The Man Who Knew Too Much*, and it is the very basis of *The Wrong Man*.

These signs may justifiably be seen as the workings of chance, but this is in no way irreconcilable—quite the contrary—with Christian dogma. As for the devil, it is not difficult to recognize him under the aspect of Bruno, with whom we have just dealt; but his other incarnations—the housekeeper in *Rebecca,* Uncle Charlie, Sebastian, Milly—are light years away from the Mephisto of operettas. These are not so much demons as people who are "possessed." They are always offered a chance; they preserve their human ambiguity.

This simultaneous presence of Good and Evil in the same person does not, however, constitute the mainspring of the drama, as it does in classical tragedy. Though Hitchcock's protagonists participate simultaneously in guilt and in innocence, it is impossible to discern the exact point at which these two extreme poles are balanced. Each of these two forces, the positive and the negative, seems to grow not inversely but proportionately; the guilt of the innocent will increase in proportion to his absolute innocence and vice versa. Or at least, if this strange state of equilibrium is never actually reached, we are made to glimpse it as a possibility, an asymptote against which all our good or evil resolutions will come up, and which defines the constitutive—or let us rather say the *original*—flaw in our natures. If free will manages to find its point of impact on the curve and more or less deflect its course, this can only be due to a miracle. And it is indeed a miracle, the miracle of Grace as much as of free will.

This moral universe—a thousand times more perilous, if not more fatal, than that of ancient tragedy—to which the best of the American films refer either implicitly or explicitly, provides us with a second characteristic that bears the mark of Christianity. This is the notion of *community in sin,* the ethical or religious *recto* of that which, in the form of "transfer" we have often seen as the esthetic and psychological *verso.* This right side of the coin is not completely unfamiliar to us. In *Under Capricorn,* Henrietta assumes not only the actual but also the moral crime of her husband. Similarly, the final image of *Rope* shows us the professor associated with the two criminals in the anguished wait for the moment in which the sirens will stop, shows him accepting the burden of a remorse that his students are incapable of feeling.

Each being has need of the mirror of somebody else's conscience; but in this universe where salvation shines only when illuminated by the light of Grace, he sees in that mirror only his own deformed and exposed image. The suspicion he directs against his counterpart turns back like a boomerang and overwhelms him with shame. He is perpetually taking on a responsibility not his own, and in the very act of doing so, being returned to his own solitude. This is the essence of the tragedy—a tragedy which, born of looks, gestures, and silences, owes everything to the direction, to the music with which Hitchcock skillfully seasons his librettos.

In the present instance the libretto came from a very mediocre source—a forgotten melodrama by the forgotten French playwright Paul Anthelme, which Louis Verneuil unearthed one fine day. But Hitchcock made some important changes in the play. For the first time since *Shadow of a Doubt* he did not call on his professional scenario writers but on a Catholic novelist, Paul Tabori, and on a dramatist, William Archibald, who had just completed a stage adaptation of Henry James's *Turn of the Screw.*

Keller (O. E. Hasse), the sexton of a Quebec church, has committed a murder to cover a theft. He confesses to the curate, Father Michael Logan (Montgomery Clift). As it happens, the murdered man was a lawyer named Villette, who had surprised the priest, before his ordination, in the company of a married woman

Montgomery Clift as a priest who is the prisoner to the secret of the confessional is cleared of the charge of murder when the killer's wife (Dolly Haas) avows her husband's guilt in *I Confess* (1952). (PHOTO COURTESY OF THE MUSEUM OF MODERN ART)

(Anne Baxter) and was trying to blackmail him. Father Michael commits a few blunders that turn suspicion against him.

Before going any further, let us join Jacques Rivette in emphasizing the idea of *confession,* already encountered in *Under Capricorn.* "The guilty person understands by remission of sin that he is totally discharged of it, and that his confessor is obliged, if necessary, to take the sin on himself and expiate it in his place. (Vigny, in his notes for *Cinq-Mars,* also united the confessor to the friend, to the accomplice) . . . In a variety of manners, the couples obsessed by guilt (the heart of all Hitchcock's films) live through the same experience: they manage to make the sin hesitate between two souls until it is abolished by the irremediable confusion of their destinies."

The question posed here is not whether or not the priest will keep the secret of the confessional. Nor is it a question of a Corneille-like conflict between a sworn oath and temptation, or the excuses of circumstances. Even as he experiences physical fear, which in this film constitutes the external mechanism of the "suspense"—actually, suspense is pushed into the background— Father Michael experiences a sort of vertigo in recognizing his feelings of guilt. As we have noted, the just man assumes another man's guilt to the very extent that he himself is innocent. But perhaps this innocence is only superficial.

Our hero is not absolutely pure, if only because he exposes himself to calumny. As a priest, he is no longer a man like other men. Ordination has erased his past, just as baptism has erased original sin. Now it is this very past with which the world, the police, and the law reproach him. His sin, if sin there is, is not that he has been a man before becoming a man of God, but, on the contrary, to have given way to the intimidation, the blackmail, of wanting to redeem by heroic and paradoxical conduct what need no longer be redeemed: to give way to the temptation of martyrdom. We find ourselves confronted not only with an allegory of the Fall but with a tragic situation worthy of that adjective and having as its mainspring, as in the novels of Georges Bernanos, the traps of sacrifice and sainthood.

It has been charged that the story is improbable. Couldn't Father Michael find some expedient? We can only be certain that he doesn't *want* to. Is he behaving like a saint, or like a man of overweening pride? The auteur does not say. It is not the tragic poet's business to judge his characters, not man's business to judge his fellows. And besides, this past—the weight of which is always so heavy in Hitchcock, whether it recalls the pages of Genesis or of Platonic "reminiscence"—this past is disclosed by a magnificent flashback, to the sound of Dimitri Tiomkin's music, by winding paths so enchanting that we cede to the fascination of its carnal grace. We sense that between it and the present there is a discord that must at any price be resolved, stifled, before the mechanism goes into action.

It is this mechanism that the police inspector takes pleasure in setting in motion, and the same is true of the prosecutor on the day of the trial. If Father Michael, he points out, could in an angry moment have struck Villette because he was insulting a woman, why—in another angry moment, when both this woman's reputation and Father Michael's were at stake—would the priest have resisted the temptation to kill him? Father Michael has no reply. Nevertheless, in the absence of material proof he is acquitted by the jury. It is at this moment that his true Calvary begins. The crowd will not accept the verdict. Walking in dignity through the hooting populace, the priest, who does not even have the recourse of washing his shame away, slowly leaves the courtroom. We see him surrounded by hostile faces, descending the great stairway all alone, like Christ carrying his cross. Then, below, there is a scuffle; again like Christ, he falls, his elbow starring the pane of glass on an automobile.

It is at this moment that God replies—or at least everything happens as though such were the case. A woman, Keller's wife, cries out, validating by a second avowal her husband's original confession—which, since it was not followed by a desire for atonement, was mere blasphemy. Keller flees. The film ends with a classical chase magnified by the heroism of Father Michael, who at the risk of his life tries to save the sexton, and by the latter's terrible reply that the priest is even more unfortunate than he, Keller, is, since everybody has abandoned him. He would be better off dead.

From a formal point of view, this work is no less rigorous than its predecessor, even though dialogue plays a much larger part in it. The key to its symbolism is not furnished by geometric entities but by the familiar iconography which we noted earlier: that of the *stations of the cross*. There is something of the religious chromo in this imagery, but this affected product of a bigoted Canada is decanted by Hitchcock—with the help of Robert Burks, who after *Strangers on a Train* was promoted to Hitchcock's official cameraman—with the same ease with which he decanted melodrama. A constant preference for low-angle shots gives the characters and the decor the necessary majesty. The rhythm is slower; there are fewer cuts; the camera follows the principal character, whose progress is the very leitmotif of the film.

In the two most beautiful scenes the advantages of the continuous take and the use of montage are combined with superior artistry. One of these scenes, already cited, is the departure from the court. The other takes place in the church, shortly before Father Michael's arrest. The camera accompanies the priest as he walks down the nave toward the altar on which Keller is placing some flowers. The sexton, caught by the lens in a close-up along the way, looks at him and calls: a reverse-field shot, with a continuity that is all but seamless and admirably audacious; another track shot while the two men follow each other to the sacristy. Keller halts Father Michael: new close-ups. Looks that betray fear, which increases as each discovers it in the other. The glassy look of the sexton, hiding his terror under the mask of sarcasm; the hard and proud look of the priest, but a look already briefly shot through by the terror the other man believes he reads in him. Looks charged with the densest significance, heavy with an unfathomable vertigo, worthy counterparts of Ingrid Bergman's look in *Under Capricorn*.

Glances are actually what Hitchcock uses all through the film as the basic threads of his web, the conducting canals through which the overflow of consciences is drained: the look of the inspector (Karl Malden), who watches the meeting between the priest and the wife of the counsellor with a single eye, the other being hidden by the head of his interlocutor; the look in the courtroom of Keller's wife, who is already on the verge of confession; Father Michael's look during the questioning, the trial, and in the final scene . . . In this story, in which the lips of the hero are voluntarily sealed, only these looks give us access to the mysteries of his thought. They are the most worthy and faithful messengers of the soul.

We are not to be blamed if the tone of our commentary is somewhat inflated. The majesty of this film invites as much, and leaves little room for humor. There is at most only one brief, satiric notation—the questioning of the two schoolgirls—and a few incidents that are more unusual and disquieting than comic: the fall of the bicycle and the sudden appearance of the bouquet of flowers carried by Keller as Anne Baxter leaves the church. Like the monsters with which painters peopled their "Temptation of Saint Anthony," they are the grains of sand in the too-well-greased gears, and they reveal the presence of a malevolent, diabolic concern more than they symbolize the quotidian derision of fate.

As for the glass that the prosecutor balances on his forehead, it is not pushing the text too far to see in it a no less derisive allegory of human justice. Faced with this film, it is best that we remain serious. If we insist on laughing—as is our right—Hitchcock has elsewhere furnished us, and will again, many other charming occasions.

The Third Dimension
Dial M for Murder (1954)

While *I Confess* was not a disaster, it was not as successful as its director had hoped it would be. Hitchcock was less surprised than on previous occasions. He understood that those who liked his work liked it for the wrong reasons. At first he planned to return to the old Gaumont–British formula, but he hadn't the heart or the perversity. Happily, a new stage in his career was to begin: he had just signed a contract with Paramount. This move enabled him to meet John Michael Hayes, a brilliant young playwright and occasional screenwriter, who reawakened his taste for humor—so much so that the auteur of *I Confess* decided to make a series of caustic, somewhat disdainful films that leavened sincerity with commercial necessity. Before starting on the first of these, Hitch, who felt guilty about having made Warner Brothers lose money on *Under Capricorn*, undertook to help the company with its experiments in 3-D, based on a method of binocular relief. But the life of the technique was so brief that *Dial M for Murder* was shown in France as a regular film, the necessary Polaroid glasses being no longer in use.

Nevertheless, the experiment remains an interesting one. Though the impression of 3-D is considerably lessened without the glasses, the auteur's intentions are just as clear, and at crucial moments the effect is almost as sharp. Two explicit goals can be distinguished. The first is to make the crime more gripping: while the killer tries to strangle Grace Kelly, she pivots, bends, and with her shoulders touching the table stretches her arm behind her to grasp the scissors placed at the near end of the field. She plunges them into the back of her assailant, who pivots in turn and falls backward toward the lens and onto the scissors. The other objective of the technique is to allow Hitchcock to draw attention to a certain key, which is also to be part of the problem in detection.

Finally, there is also a third intention at work, but this one is less evident: to enclose the actors in a sealed, theatrical world, to give the spectator—the camera having most often been placed in a pit—the view he might get from an orchestra seat.

The fact of the matter is that this film, like *Rope*, was adapted from a successful play (by Frederick Knott), and as was true of *Rope*, though little was changed, it is nonetheless quite Hitchcockian. A former tennis champion (Ray Milland), eager to get rid of his wife, pays a killer over whom he has a blackmail hold, to break into his apartment disguised as a robber. But in the scene we have just mentioned, the murderer is transformed into the victim. Undiscouraged, the husband turns to the police and has little trouble persuading them that his wife wanted to do away with a blackmailer. A letter from her lover, as well as a few other objects he manages to slip into the dead man's pocket, point the police on the path he wants them to follow. But the evening before the execution (we are in England), thanks to the flair of an inspector and despite gaffes by the lover (Robert Cummings), a hack mystery writer, the matter of the key turns against him. The entire last part of the film is nothing more than an exposition of the reasoning involved, yet one's attention never flags. This is because the solution is given to us by the very configuration of the setting. The algebraic formula of the stage play is here given a geometric expression of rare elegance. The point is not so much to split hairs as to make us see things clearly—to see in the way Hitchcock wants us to see.

But in this film the director's art does not consist only in making abstract data interesting—in line with this we might recall the mastery with which Hitchcock, at the beginning of the story, presents a ten-minute conversation between two motionless men without trying our patience. Though the plot development is mathematically spare, the characters are not treated like mathematical entities. The husband is ignoble but charming, and never loses his composure even when finally unmasked. As for the lover, he is a complete caricature, and the wife is as dumb as she is pretty. A playful caricature, one might say, by that good Englishman Hitchcock has always been, because the fact is they are both American. But above and beyond this rather superficial desire to satirize, this choice of characters has a much more profound significance and follows our auteur's habit of presenting Evil in an attractive guise. The heroine herself gives way to this fascination: still perhaps in love with her husband, she is overwhelmed by the revelation of a foulness she was far from suspecting, but which nevertheless adds to his stature in her eyes.

We cannot sufficiently admire the appearance behind the panes on the morning of the final confrontation of the slim silhouette in the pale light of the garden; the same goes for the anguished wait in the chiaroscuro of the room with its drawn blinds.

It is by such observations of time or light, by some half-concealed tears, by some gestures of impatience or lassitude, that Hitchcock softens the somewhat rigid mathematics of his discourse, makes poetry spring out from an unexpected turn of the road, and adds a new dimension to his work. The lesson of *Rope* continues to bear fruit. Grace Kelly, though she is no less badly treated in *Dial M for Murder* than in the two following films, is in some way more tender and more touching here, has something that makes her the younger sister of Joan Fontaine.

Despite these touches of sadness, which are almost an after-

thought, we are nevertheless far removed from the qualities of pathos in *I Confess*. Hitchcock has changed registers. It is comedy he has his eye on.

The Matrix-Figure
Rear Window (1954)

And *Rear Window* is half comedy. It is without doubt one of Hitchcock's most profound films, but its profundity accords with

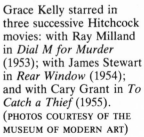

Grace Kelly starred in
three successive Hitchcock
movies: with Ray Milland
in *Dial M for Murder*
(1953); with James Stewart
in *Rear Window* (1954);
and with Cary Grant in *To
Catch a Thief* (1955).
(PHOTOS COURTESY OF THE
MUSEUM OF MODERN ART)

the unremitting irony of its tone. As we know, the Hitchcock team
was enriched by the addition of a new official collaborator: John
Michael Hayes. It is largely to his incisive, cynical—not to say
nasty—dialogue that the films of this period are to owe their
obvious relationship to one another.

But first let us consider the data. It is in *Rear Window* that the
deductive aspect we drew attention to in relation to *Strangers on a
Train* is presented in its purest form. The formal postulate is of a
simplicity that implies so many possible meanings that its very
statement presupposes that we have chosen among them. To begin
in the most modest and objective way possible, let us merely say
that the theme concerns the very essence of cinema, which is
seeing, spectacle. A man watches and waits while we watch this
man and wait for what he is waiting for. A celebrated shot in
Robert Flaherty's *Nanook,* the one in which the eskimo lies in wait
for the walrus that will surge from the end of the visual field, had
previously enabled us to enter into the same state of grace. But
here an entire work is deliberately constructed on what in
Flaherty's documentary was only a fugitive, accidental beauty. We
are constantly splitting ourselves in two while the protagonist of
the film splits himself in two, constantly identifying with him while
he is identifying with the man he is spying on.

If ever the word metaphysic could fearlessly be used about a
Hitchcock film, it would certainly be about this one. But this isn't
only a reflexive, critical work in the Kantian sense of the word.
This theory of spectacle implies a theory of space, and that in turn
implies a moral idea which necessarily—apodictically, as is said in
philosophy—derives from it. With one masterly stroke, Hitchcock
has here designed the key construct of his entire work, and every
one of his other blueprints is probably a corollary, an individual
example of this "matrix-figure." We are at the intersecting point of
all the material and moral dominants of Hitchcockian mythology,
at the heart of a problem whose elegant solution has yet to be
found.

A news photographer (James Stewart) with a broken leg tries to
while away the time by watching the spectacle visible from his
window. Armed with a telescopic lens, he has noticed the strange

behavior of one of his neighbors. With the help of a few facts and a great deal of ingenuity, he eventually deduces that this neighbor has just killed his wife. After this his enforced immobility is transformed into the most exciting adventure. He waits, hoping that events will justify his deductions. We wait, hoping along with him. In a manner of speaking, the crime is desired by the man who expects to make of his discovery his supreme delectation, the very sense of his life. The crime is desired by us, the spectators, who fear nothing so much as seeing our hopes deceived.

This is not the first time that Hitchcock has drawn attention to such sadistic expectations on the part of the public, whether he cheats it with a phony happy ending or overwhelms it with an event whose cruelty is unexpected just because it might too easily have been foreseen. But what has until now been only an embellishment here becomes the load-bearing beam of the entire framework.

The thread of deduction, followed to the end, leads the photographer to extremes. The passion to know, or more exactly to see, will end by suffocating all other feelings. The highest pleasure of this "voyeur" will coincide with the apex of his fear. His punishment will be that his own fiancée, a few yards away, but separated by the space of the courtyard, will be surprised in the suspect's apartment. But no matter how profound this motif, it is only one of the fibers of a sheaf. Parallel to this line, which could be called that of *indiscretion,* run at least two other major themes.

The first is that of *solitude.* This idea is made concrete on the one hand by the photographer's inability to move from his wheelchair, and on the other by the group of well-separated rabbit hutches that are the apartments he can see from his window. Realistic, indeed caricatural, this latter motif provides an opportunity to paint several of the types of fauna flourishing in Greenwich Village in particular and a big city in general. A sealed world inside that other sealed world represented by the City, which can be seen through the gap of a narrow alley, it is made up of a given number of small sealed worlds that differ from Leibnitz's monads in that they have windows and, because of this, exist not as things in themselves but as pure representations. Everything

happens as though they were the projections of the voyeur's
thoughts—or desires; he will never be able to find in them more
than he had put there, more than he hopes for or is waiting for. On
the facing wall, separated from him by the space of the courtyard,
the strange silhouettes are like so many shadows in a new version
of Plato's cave. Turning his back to the true sun, the photographer
loses the ability to look Being in the face. We risk this interpretation because it is supported by the ever-present Platonism in
Hitchcock's work. As is true of Edgar Allan Poe's stories, this
work is constructed on the implicit base of a philosophy of *Ideas*.
Here, the idea—even if it be only the pure idea of Space, Time, or
Desire—precedes existence and substance.

But this allegory of knowledge is enriched by the intrusion of a
third anecdotal element, the love story of the photographer and
his fiancée (Grace Kelly). It is enriched by a moral symbol—one
might even say a *theological* symbol. As will be true in *The Wrong
Man*—and much more than was true in *I Confess*—this is a
Hitchcock work whose significance cannot be grasped without
precise reference to Christian dogma. In fact, we are invited to do
this by three Biblical citations inserted in the web of the dialogue.
Jansenist or Augustinian rather than puritanical, this fable denounces not only the *libido sciendi*—all the easier to identify in
that here as in Genesis it is provoked by the curiosity of
Woman—but what the Fathers of the Church have called
delectatio morosa. To the idea of physical solitude is grafted that of
moral solitude, conceived as the punishment for that hypertrophy
of desire.

Neither the reporter nor his fiancée want to see that paradise
which they insist on believing lost and which is nevertheless very
close to them, as is indicated—among other signs—by the bouquet
that transforms the invalid's room into a flower garden: there are
fugitive moments in life when poetry can blossom even in a sewer.
Their solitude echoes that of the spinster resolutely seeking escape
in fantasy, that of the childless couple, that of the young
newlyweds submerged in the sexual passion of the first days of
marriage. Hitchcock is not a censor of the flesh but of the desire

whose constitutive vice is to feed on itself and forget the love which must serve as its base. The world he denounces is, on the contrary, the hypocritical world of Victorian society. If the hungry kisses with which Grace Kelly covers James Stewart's bored face have something obscene about them, it is because the photographer, whose impotence is not so much physical as moral, is incapable of replying to them with equal ardor. In short, each of the characters—protagonists or those playing a minor role—is enclosed not only in the cell of his apartment, but in the stubborn satisfaction of something which when seen externally, partially, and from afar can only appear ludicrous.

All these themes mutually serve as counterpoints, and as is only right in a work so rigorously elaborated, there comes a moment in which they crystalize in a single perfect accord: the death of the little dog. A bothersome witness, the animal has just been done away with by the murderer. Its owner goes to the window and utters a searing shriek, following which lights go on in all the windows except that of the murderer, whose presence can be discerned only by the red tip (note the utilization of color's expressive power) of his glowing cigarette. This scene—as are all the scenes in the film—is tinged with mockery. A dog is only a dog, and under the circumstances the words spoken by the woman ("You don't know the meaning of the word neighbor") invite laughter. But in this world of appearances, of inauthenticity, the most atrocious tragedy takes on the mask of the ridiculous. The dog is the gimcrack repetition of that "innocent" who, as in Sabotage or the merry-go-round scene in Strangers on a Train, might have been a child: as it happens, the dog-owning couple is childless.

The important thing is that because of the woman's words, once the reaction gets underway, each of these people will drink the cup of his egoism down to the lees. As we have previously indicated, not only will the highpoint of the photographer's pleasure coincide with that of his greatest anguish and his discovery of his responsibility—because it is someone else, in the person of his fiancée, whom he has exposed to danger—but in his talk with the murderer, who suddenly appears in his apartment, he does not even have the satisfaction of playing the sympathetic role.

"What do you want of me?" the murderer asks him, attributing the reason for the photographer's investigation to the most despicable motive, blackmail—a motive which is, however, less despicable than the real one: idle curiosity.

This film is one of those that best illustrates the cardinal virtue of Hitchcockian morality: *exigence*. We can never be hard enough on ourselves—such is its lesson. Evil hides not only under the appearance of Good, but in our most casual and innocent acts, those we think have no ethical significance, those which in principle involve no responsibility. The criminals in this universe are attractively portrayed only so that they can better denounce the Pilates, which in one way or another we all are.

It will be said that Hitchcock never goes beyond this simple denunciation: he severely scourges our egoism, but he doesn't really care to indicate the way out of it. The blasé irony of the ending in this film clearly supports this severe principle. A last shot shows our couple just as they were, as though nothing had happened.

Hitchcock may be a moralist, but there is nothing of the moralizer about him. As we have said, this is not his concern. His role is only to illuminate the situation and let everybody draw his own conclusions. And then too, this guilt which he is so skillful in bringing to the surface is perhaps less of a moral than of a metaphysical order. It is, as we have said—and let's not hesitate to repeat it—part of our very nature, the heritage of original sin. This is so much the case that without reference to Christian dogma, to the idea of Grace, the pessimism of this attitude would rightly make us angry, just as it irritates all those who try to base morality on human values alone. For Hitchcock, too, the heart of man is "hollow and a sink of iniquity"; those who reject this image can do so only from the viewpoint of atheistic angelism, thereby recognizing the logic of our interpretation. It is paradoxical, to say the least, to smile when offered theological keys to the work of our cineast and nevertheless to continue heaping upon him the same invective with which Christianity is attacked elsewhere.

Flowers of Rhetoric
To Catch a Thief (1955)

At the beginning of summer 1954, Hitch flew to France and, using the new Vistavision technique, filmed the location scenes of *To Catch a Thief* on the Côte d'Azur.

Everything in this "private joke" taken from a novel by David Dodge is redolent of vacation, of fantasy. The satire is still acid, but once its goal is attained it relaxes into a smile and not a grimace. Only eccentricities, not deep vices, are laughed at—or at least so it seems, because we have learned not to put too much trust in appearances. When questioned by reporters, Hitchcock spoke only of his return to the humor of the English films. It is a gastronomical tour, with merely the pinch of "suspense" necessary to bring out the flavor of the dishes.

The "falsely accused" of this romantic fairytale is no longer involved in murder but in theft. John Robie (Cary Grant), a gentleman thief, is enjoying a cozy retirement in his Côte d'Azur villa, a retirement that is in no way due to repentance. Suddenly there is a new outbreak of thefts in which the technique formerly perfected by the ex-"Cat" is used. To clear himself of suspicion, Robie has no recourse but to unmask his disciple by outdoing him, even at the risk of setting at his heels both the police and the justly alarmed confederates of the new "cat." The game is a dangerous one, but at least it wins our hero the heart of a rich American heiress (Grace Kelly), who obstinately insists on taking him for what he no longer is. Needless to say, he is not in too much of a hurry to disabuse her, since her error lends him a kind of cynical grace and permits him to play the moralist without being too heavy about it. A single, almost embarrassing, moment of cruelty—the one at the cemetery in which Robie, indignant at being publicly accused by the daughter (Brigitte Auber) of his former confederate, very cavalierly slaps her. Hitchcock, too, plays cat and mouse—with the feelings of the public; and he knows just how close one of his most sympathetic heroes can come to displeasing that public. Once the mystery has been cleared up, he will know how to shame us for our indulgence of Robie by revealing that he is not a lout but a defender of the widow and the orphan. The athletic young girl is actually the "cat." It was she whom this professor-in-spite-of-himself had suspected all along.

Several familiar themes will be apparent in this summary: that of the power of the past, that of suspicion, that of responsibility, that of the exchange, and even that of an almost total identification with somebody else. Brigitte Auber copies Grant's feline behavior and even his striped jersey; though guilty, she usurps the pity due to innocence; though innocent, he does not object to any of the aces that the fact of being thought guilty slips into the hand he is playing. This sun-flooded vacation is a vacation from morality. Hitchcock, breaking for once with his taste for extremes, gives us an average, balanced example of his well-known formula of transmutation. Of all the innocents in the Hitchcockian menagerie, Robie is the one whose false guilt is most lightly borne. This is because of them all he is the least innocent. "Why should I steal?" he asks the Lloyd's investigator. "I'm rich." "How did you become rich?" "By stealing." But as the conversation continues, the good detective becomes aware that his own honesty is perhaps no less impure. There is a potential transfer, but one might as well try to analyze a sunbeam.

As for its form, *To Catch a Thief* offers a charming potpourri of the themes—including the musical themes of the score—of the American period, just as *Saboteur* did of the English period. There is no well-defined formal challenge. We are reminded of a concertante style—with each voice in turn making its own melody heard—rather than of the dense texture of a canon, or a highly complex fugue. And the "cadences" are numerous—bravura sections that are not simply exercises in cinematic acrobatics but a splendid visual festival. This is how we perceive the helicopter flight over the Corniche, the flower-market battle, the fireworks display—to which we will return—and finally the masked ball, a masterpiece of deliberate bad taste over which the director is not afraid to linger a bit at the decisive moment of the story, thus infringing the conventional laws of "suspense." Hitchcock, who has been so praised—a little superficially—for being above all a good storyteller, here shows his clear desire—and this tendency will be confirmed in future films—to keep the story in the background. Despite the "discoveries" and "disclosures" in the film, scarcely a fourth of which was shot on location, there is a dominant documentary, almost neo-realistic, tone that constitutes its chief attraction and novelty.

Even the performances partake of this freedom. The mimicry of the actors—remember the scene in the water—has an unusual air of improvisation about it. But this charming relaxation in no way destroys the unity of style. Under the blue Mediterranean sky, this mosaic of bright colors never stumbles into dissonance. At the desired moment, this zig-zagging fantasia returns to a basic tonality, no matter how many the number and incongruity of the modulations. In this game of "cat and mouse," the theme of the chase constitutes the basic line on which will be perched, like so many bouquets, an abundance of cinematic set pieces. Since we cannot enumerate all these embellishments—which are like the embellishments of eighteenth-century music—we will cite only three of the most dazzling. They would merit a leading place in any glossary of Hitchcockian flowers of rhetoric.

The first is a simple *image*. It lasts only a fraction of a second and its metaphorical sense is not even hinted at. It is the image of a cigarette stubbed out in an egg. We have a foreshadowing of this in *Rebecca*—the cigarette that time being put out in a jar of cold cream—but here the presence of *color* strangely reinforces the strength of the impression. The fact is that Hitchcock is one of the few film-makers for whom color is an auxiliary and not a shackle, who keeps it from being a servile imitation of painting. Many images in *To Catch a Thief* are not free of cacophony, but these dissonances ought not to shock us more than do those in nature. Though "picture postcard" views abound, there are no more in this film than might be seen on a drive from Cannes to Menton. Consider also that in a painter, color is endowed with an existence anterior to the object, if it can be put that way. Promoted to the dignity of being, "blue" will be the common denominator of the sea, an eye, or a dress. In the movies, on the other hand, color is not an end but a means of providing a particular object with a supplementary degree of reality. It is to this that we owe the sharp sense of the concrete. A black and white image would not have been able to provoke the strong impression created here by the yellow and sticky substance of the egg.

What does this "gag" mean? Nothing and everything. It is designed to provoke both discomfort and laughter. It is extraordinary, but it is not extraordinary in the way surrealists use the extraordinary—as a matter of principle. Like the fall of the bicycle in *I Confess,* it expresses the idea of the inimicalness, of the fundamental resistance, of things. And Hitchcock, as his talent matures, will go on multiplying these observations. Through them, he shows us that he is one of the greatest inventors the screen has ever known, an inventor not so much of "gags" as of forms. By this is to be understood cinematic forms which not only refer to geometry but to that part of mathematical science called "rational dynamics." These schemas are motor-schemas endowed with a dual spatial and temporal quality. To describe them by abstracting one from the other would be to falsify them.

The second embellishment, the cross-cutting between the fireworks and the love scene, is a true comparison. As we know, Eisenstein devoted part of his experiments and writings to the task of discovering a cinematic equivalent of the poets' metaphor. For several years now the famous theory of the "montage of attractions," long discarded, was in the process of being revivified. The planetarium sequence in *Rebel Without a Cause,* the most beautiful moments of Rossellini's *La Paura* and *Italian Journey,* show in conjunction two series of facts that have only a purely poetic relationship. We can similarly be thankful to Hitchcock for having by means of these bouquets of fire—in an accelerated montage of closer and closer shots—symbolized an amorous embrace with more lightness and humor than Eisenstein, the auteur of *The General Line,* had been able to achieve in his rustic wedding scene. Old stuff? Old enough to be able to emerge from its attic and shake off the encrusted dust of naiveté and pedanticism. It is better to rummage in the chests of yesteryear than in the trashbaskets of yesterday.

The third jewel is an ellipsis, by means of which this fireworks scene is joined to the next. The fireworks are over. We've scarcely had time to note Grace Kelly dozing on her couch and Cary Grant re-entering his room. A door opens and Grace Kelly enters Robie's room demanding that he return her mother's jewels! It is as if we were emerging from a heavy sleep, which seems to have lasted only a second. Suddenly we are aware of all the time that's gone by. The liaison is extremely simple, but somebody had to have the audacity to think of it. Hitchcock comes up with tens, hundreds, of these effects which seem so simple once they've been thought of. Caught up in the heat of the action, we don't notice the beauty of the seam that Hitchcock, when he wants to, is more skillful than anyone in rendering invisible. If the seam sometimes appears to stand out more than necessary, let's not be fooled: he is counting, as we will see in *The Man Who Knew Too Much,* on its being noticed.

Is He Good or Bad?
The Trouble with Harry (1956)

For some time now Hitchcock had been producing half-hour films for television. Those that he directed himself allowed him to tell stories that he liked but could not make films of. He also had the opportunity to train several young directors such as John Meredyth Lucas and Robert Stevens. These television films are not very important in the body of his work. Nevertheless, several of them clearly bear his brand—for example, the first, *Revenge,* which recounts the tribulations of a nice guy whose wife is a mythomaniac. One evening he finds her prostrate in the kitchen, and she claims to have been raped by an unknown intruder. The couple race through the town in search of the satyr. Suddenly she points her finger at a passerby and shrieks: "That's him!" The husband attacks the man with an iron rod. On the way home the wife once more points at a passerby: "That's him!"

This rather ghastly story is told with a precision and brilliance that is in no way hindered by the simple and economical television technique. Rumor has it that others of these short films are equally well done. They would have to be judged individually.

Thanks to this experience, Hitchcock decided to make a feature film by adapting television methods to the cinema. No sooner said than done. "I finished *To Catch a Thief*," he tells us, "one afternoon at five-thirty, and by seven-thirty *Harry* was underway." The reason for this haste was that the exteriors of this new film had to be shot during a very short and very precise time lapse: the one in which leaves turn from green to yellow to red before their autumnal fall from the trees.

Taken from a novel by John Trevor Story, *The Trouble with Harry* is an extremely faithful adaptation. The only notable difference is that in the novel there is no mention of the police. John Michael Hayes's dialogue faithfully reproduces the original dialogue. Where then is Hitchcock's hand? In the direction? No doubt; yet none of his works is more spare, and the paucity of effects contrasts strangely with their abundance in the previous film. To tell the truth, there is scarcely more than one effect, and that is of a completely static nature: a foreshortened shot of the corpse's immense feet and red socks. By and large the dialogue carries most of the burden.

Where then is Hitchcock's hand? Nowhere, if the film is to be analyzed in this manner. Everywhere, for those who go to see it without worrying their heads about the problem. The fact is that this film, disliked in the United States, is the one which in France did most for its director's reputation. After this film, people were willing to recognize him as an auteur rather than a mere technician. If Hitchcock changed little in this story, it's because he didn't have to, for it was already sufficiently Hitchcockian. The number of Hitchcockian stories in the world is certainly very great: a good third, if not a half, of all those that have been written until now—and that is if we consider only fiction, since *The Wrong Man* will show us that there are also Hitchcockian stories in the daily newspaper. This is not said to diminish Hitchcock's merit or originality. On the contrary. His point of view corresponds to one of the two or three (we might go so far as five or six, but the

In *The Trouble with Harry* (1956) the corpse of Shirley MacLaine's husband means little more to the inhabitants of a small town than a troublesome object to be disposed of. (PHOTO COURTESY OF THE MUSEUM OF MODERN ART)

number is not infinite) *possible* esthetic or moral positions. His humor is one of the two or three forms of humor possible. His strength comes from this very universality.

Having said this, let's acknowledge that this new work is a perfect example of that macabre Anglo-Saxon humor which in England itself has failed to find a director (let's not say scenario writer) worthy of it. It is a humor that can be compared with that of Swift or Thomas De Quincey, or with that of the *New Yorker* cartoonists Charles Addams and Saul Steinberg, who in point of fact illustrated the credits for *The Trouble with Harry*. Or it could be compared to that of Mark Twain: the little boy in the film for whom today is tomorrow since yesterday was today and tomorrow will be yesterday is just like the American humorist's character who is no longer very sure whether it was he or his twin brother who was long ago drowned in the bathtub.

There is more. The theme of transfer, carried to the point of the absurd, can be recognized with particular ease. The characters are not innocent people who are believed to be guilty: they themselves believe they are guilty; they want to be.

A corpse lies under the purpling foliage of a Vermont wood. All those who successively come across it not only congratulate themselves on this death but claim the authorship of it. The "captain," a retired sailor picturesquely played by Edmund Gwenn, talks of a clumsy hunting shot; the unfortunate Harry's wife (Shirley MacLaine), of a bottle with which she struck him the previous evening; a spinster, of a heel with which she hit him. As for the others—an irritatingly argumentative boy, a modernist painter, a myopic doctor—they all contemplate the corpse indifferently and offer their help in getting rid of it. The doctor, whom it is possible to take for a madman, diagnoses heart failure, which might very well have been brought on by the rifle fire and the two attacks on Harry. Who's to know the truth? And besides, what difference does it make? This humor, like that of Kafka, whom we will mention again in dealing with *The Wrong Man,* is based on the idea of the absurd.

The story then is even more amoral than that of *To Catch a Thief.* As Jean Domarchi notes, everything takes place as though the characters had undergone an "ablation of conscience." Insofar as they are concerned, the corpse has absolutely no significance: it is only a compromising object that has to be gotten rid of. "The most curious thing about this film," said Jacques Rivette, "is that it is impossible to decide whether its characters are or are not 'good' or 'bad'; but perhaps they are beyond such a distinction?"

The disdain with which the auteur loads his characters splashes onto the spectators no less strongly than it did in the two preceding works. Just as in *Rear Window* we would have been disappointed to find that the crime committed in the apartment across the courtyard was only the fruit of the photographer's imagination, here we join the characters in their pleasure over poor Harry's death. The comic mode allows the auteur to solicit our complicity more than he had been able to do previously. We ourselves are no better than these shoddy or cynical beings.

Of all Hitchcock's works, this one undoubtedly has the raciest dialogue, the most scandalous situations, and the most (with the exception of *Lifeboat*) misanthropic point of view. Deliberately negative, it shows us the obverse of the coin without indicating to us, as elsewhere, that it *is* only the obverse; it even lacks the idea of fascination, of vertigo, or of danger. It is the film in which the characters are most lacking in flesh and in which they always behave like marionettes. It should also be said that it is pure *comedy*—the second American one, after *Mr. and Mrs. Smith*— the only one which the wily auteur, who has a careful eye and is fertile in "gags," has treated in a consistently successful manner.

We have noted that the direction was particularly restrained. If we consider only the shooting script—devoid of all attempts at artfulness—the talky dialogue, and the sometimes free, sometimes emphatic acting, this film very effectively conveys the impression of something done for television. However, let's not talk of the absence of style but rather of a new purpose, a new formal challenge analogous to that of *Dial M For Murder*. The important thing is that from a most unpromising postulate the director has obtained the most charming effects. Against a deliberately flat background, the least object, the least gesture, is thrown into relief, and we read Hitchcock like an open book. Unlike many others, he has no need to "play cinema" to amuse us. He's never bored, and he never bores us. He *is* cinema no matter what he does. In this film there is finally a door through which rushes all that great poetry whose absence, quite exceptionally, we deplored in *Lifeboat* and some of the English films. The splendor of this autumn landscape—the symbol of disintegration—is in no way superfluous. Since the spectacle of crimsoning forest opens and closes the film, it serves as something like a counterweight to the rather puppet-like mechanism of the farce; it is the precious element by means of which the bitterness of the moral is palliated.

Beyond "Suspense"
The Man Who Knew Too Much (1956)

The first *The Man Who Knew Too Much* having been one of the least successful films of the English period, we will not attempt an over-facile analysis by comparing it with the American version. The exact reasons (see the earlier discussion) that led Hitchcock to undertake a "remake" are unimportant. The point is that he was not content merely to improve the form, to probe the characters, or to update the story: what we are given is a veritable transfiguration. In its new form, this film is one of those in which the Hitchcockian mythology finds its purest, if not its most obvious expression. It is the film in which the construction—that famous construction based, as we have seen in discussing *Shadow of a Doubt,* on interior rhyme—is most deliberate.

The beginning, however, is of a nonchalant grace that hardly foreshadows this rigor. The touristic and gastronomic journey begun in *To Catch a Thief* continues. We are in Morocco, and the satire moves along at a good clip. Once more, Americans—average, very average, Americans—are the targets for these shafts. James Stewart lends his rubbery features to the portrayal of a doctor on vacation. The features are less slack than those of the photographer in *Rear Window,* but just a bit more stupid. The dialogue wallows in deliberate platitudes that are caught by the sallies of the direction. There is, for example, the scene in the Moroccan cafe in which Hitch offers us a demonstration of comedy based on "pure gestures": Stewart, seated like a Turk and served in local fashion—in other words, without cutlery—doesn't know what to do with his long legs and his fingers. But how can this be described? Such a feast can only be appreciated by seeing it. On the risky roads along which only the great makers of comedy have been able to stroll with honorable results, Hitchcock procedes with a surety, an elegance, worthy of Chaplin, Keaton, Cukor, or Hawks in their great days. As the plot moves along, the police— French—are also clawed along the way, and we come to a little scene of cruel humor that is no less finely etched: the doctor, fearing that his wife will have an attack of hysteria when she learns that their son has been kidnapped, forces her, by a kind of blackmail, to swallow a sedative: unless she swallows, he won't tell her a thing. Once she learns the news, the wife, as her husband watches with a half-hangdog, half-satisfied expression, bursts into tears: So that was why! He is contemptible!

This is really pure Hitchcock. However, it will be considerably more difficult to identify the famous transfer theme in the basic story, which is the same as in the English version. To tell the truth, in this film, the heart of which is of a completely allegorical nature, there is only an exchange, the exchange of a secret; as in the first version, this will be the revelation of an assassination attempt against a foreign diplomat, one who this time (after all, one has to keep up with History) is to be "liquidated" by his own government. Our couple, then, fearing for the life of their child, decide not to say a word; and taking a plane to England, they begin their own investigation as best they can. Needless to say, the doctor follows a false lead, which makes for one of the most obviously "gratuitous" scenes in all Hitchcock's work. Having misled himself into thinking that a taxidermist's shop is the wolf's lair, the doctor, blundering and irascible, is unceremoniously shown to the door as the wild beasts look on mockingly. Nevertheless, this side-dish, so unusual that it is almost surrealistic, does not spoil the menu: the "rhyme" has its logic, which the logic of the story would be wrong not to recognize. Before long we will find the true "Ambrose Chapel," a new lair peopled by tigers that are infinitely more dangerous.

It is in this Protestant church (and "Protestant" implies a new pretext for satire) that the vicar of the great conspiracy officiates. From this point on, the two versions, the English and the American, sail along side by side—which only emphasizes the difference of their riggings. Perhaps the second version has no other superiority than its formal perfection, but only when form achieves perfection—and the truth of this is not only to be found in Hitchcock but in the history of art in general—does it become significant. Beyond the basic irony there is in this film a reigning climate of gravity imputable to the very splendor of the direction.

Simply by means of its rigor, the "figure," as we shall see in discussing the Albert Hall scene, leads us directly to the idea.

Her simpleton husband having let himself be caught in the trap, the doctor's wife (Doris Day) is unable to get the police to break into the now sealed doors of Ambrose Chapel. She learns that one of the Scotland Yard detectives, who has previously promised to help her, is at Albert Hall, where he is in charge of the security of the foreign diplomat; and she has no choice but to go to the concert hall. In the meantime, we have learned—but she has not—that the assassin has received instructions to wait for a certain clash of cymbals before he fires. The orchestra leader raises his baton. The music begins, and with it the classic "suspense."

The scene is a choice one, and some people reproach Hitchcock for having overdone it. All they can see in this alternately hot and cold shower, which from second to second takes us from frank laughter to the most real terror, is a stylistic exercise; it is actually a brilliant sleight-of-hand that sometimes hides the strings by which it is worked and sometimes exposes them for all to see. But in exposing the framework of his construction this way, it is the framework itself that the auteur invites us to consider. From this point of view, that of architecture, *The Man Who Knew Too Much* seems the exact corollary of *Rear Window*. To make the transition from one to the other, it is only necessary to modify one of the terms of the formula: *Time* must be substituted for *Space*.

In *Rear Window* the character is separated from the object he desires or fears by a given area. Here, it is a no less clearly delineated interval of passing time. The gulf is no longer that of an empty courtyard but of a lapse of time—the cause of no less an anguish and an interval over which the heroine is at all costs determined to leap. Just as James Stewart was immobilized by his injured leg and used the artifice of the telescopic lens, so Doris Day is here paralyzed by her ignorance and counts, if it may be put that way, on the help of presentiment. She knows that an assassination attempt will be made, but she is unable to say when and how. In this case the event will be independent of her will but at the same time the projection of her fear, just as in the other case the murder was in some way the projection of the photographer's desire.

Continuing our comparison we see that the world in *Rear Window* is a world of contemplation, of absolute passivity, from which there is no way out. The world of *The Man Who Knew Too Much,* in which the dominant factor is time, introduces a dimension of possible action. And salvation can only be obtained through the combined interplay of Fate (but isn't it rather Providence?) and Free Will.

Our heroine, a former pop singer, has taught her son one of the tunes which brought her success. The film simultaneously affirms and denies this refrain: *Que sera, sera.* The young woman "knows too much," and because of this has lost her innocence (once more the allegory of the Fall)—in other words her instinct, the instinct that is to save her. She senses the assassination, but she wouldn't prevent it if she could, since the life of her son is at stake. However, she can't prevent herself from giving way to a kind of fear inspired by the imminence of something terrible. Her anguish is fed, as is ours, by what may perhaps be only the feeling of the inexorable, pure, flow of time. With that always superb irony, that same pitiless disdain, the auteur of *Rear Window* describes another sort of fascination, the coordinates of which are this time not of a spatial but of a temporal order; and he does this with the ease of a past master in the art of dispensing such fascination. What the heroine fears is not so much that something terrifying will happen, but that as the seconds pile up with a heavier and heavier weight, this something has not yet happened. Her paradoxical tears move us because we too are swept along. And—instinct banishing all logic, all caution—at the very moment that the cymbals are to clash, she cries out.

But this ridiculous and poignant cry with which she signals her defeat is also the first manifestation of her free will and the instrument of her final salvation, because the grateful minister invites her to the embassy where the child is being kept. This cry is both in the order of things and an expression of the revolt of her sensibility against the cold logic of the assassination plot. It is the grain of sand that will throw the wheels out of gear. It is a kind of deliverance: the counterpart of that confession whose presence we have pointed out in many previous works. All the usual Hitchcock themes are manifested here only by signs reduced to their simplest expression, and their brilliance is all the purer for those who know how to decipher them.

As we have seen, the English version concludes with a pitched battle at the end of which the mother, a markswoman, draws a bead on the chief spy as he forces the little girl along the roofs. Let us transpose this spatial and visual "gag" into a scale of time and sound: the result is the new ending. (In line with this, we should point up the importance of sound—music or a cry—in a film constructed around a clash of cymbals.)

We are at the embassy. The risk the heroine takes is that of singing the famous song and braving Fate with the same phrase that affirms its overriding power: *Que sera, sera.* The sound of the melody travels down the corridors and rises up the grand stairway, reaching in muffled form the room in which the child is dozing. He recognizes the tune, and the tenderhearted woman who has been assigned to keep an eye on him (evil destiny will be averted through the intercession of two women) suggests that he whistle it. And this whistling, the counterpart of that cry he had uttered in Ambrose Chapel, will this time find its echo.

Though the woman is the one who mediates, it is the man who will be the one to act. The father manages to leave the reception; he goes upstairs and rescues his son after a brief scuffle with the kidnapper, whom he coldbloodedly throws down the stairs.

"What will be, will be," yes; but also: "Heaven helps those who help themselves." The presence, even simultaneously, of these two adages is not enough of itself to bear witness to the depths of the work. What matters is the purity of the allegorical design that supports them. Of course, *The Man Who Knew Too Much* gets its external characteristics from a popular novel and doesn't belong to the more noble kind of *fable* represented by *Le vent souffle où il veut* (doesn't Bresson's film express the same moral under its more intellectual exterior?) and *The Wrong Man,* with which we will conclude our discussion. As we said in our commentary of *Under*

Doris Day gets a few pointers from Hitchcock during the filming of the 1956 American remake of *The Man Who Knew Too Much*, "one of the least successful films of the English period." (PHOTO COURTESY OF MUSEUM OF MODERN ART)

Capricorn, Hitchcock need only reveal the depth of his intentions once or twice for all the rest of his work to be illuminated and magnified. Should he be taken to task for having sought the approbation of the crowd? No, if in the final analysis he raises that crowd to him rather than lowers himself to it. The explanation we suggest is not one that might be given, for example, by a sociologist or a psychoanalyist who excludes all value judgments. What we offer are keys and not a surgeon's scalpel. The opening made by such keys, far from disemboweling the work, should permit it to breathe more freely, to be better understood and therefore better enjoyed.

A kind of emotion nobler than the sentimentality proper to espionage stories circulates here at the depths. Our pleasure will be increased if we learn to be sensitive to it when it wells to the surface. Hitchcock tricks us? Of course: he even makes the serious nature of his work spring out, in a most unpredictable manner, from a turn in the road.

CONCLUSION:
THE WRONG MAN (1957)

In anticipation of the joys we can confidently expect from Alfred Hitchcock, we are pleased to be able to conclude our study of him with a film that not only brings together the themes scattered throughout his work but also eloquently proves that the attempt to illuminate the depths of his work was worth the effort.

The Paramount series and the television programs had made Hitchcock more popular than ever. Convinced that he was now strong enough to face a possible commercial failure, he decided to make the sort of film his heart was set on. He therefore produced *The Wrong Man* for Warner Brothers, contenting himself with 10 percent of the boxoffice receipts, which he knew were questionable.

This obviously ambitious work[1] is not only stripped of romantic adventure but also of all "suspense." Like *Lifeboat,* it is a *fable,* but it is also the exact account of a real event reported in the newspapers. Can it be only a coincidence? This kind of apologue, often a pretext for mediocrity, is the very genre to which belong the most original recent films: *Le vent souffle où il veut, Italian Journey, Mr. Arkadin,* and *Eléna et les hommes.* In addition, Bresson, Rossellini, Welles, and Renoir were as successful as Hitchcock in manipulating the seemingly contradictory strengths

[1]Hitchcock seems to have temporarily abandoned comedy as well as John Michael Hayes. Maxwell Anderson did the scenario.

of the allegorical and the *documentary* forms (even when, as in *Eléna,* it was only a documentary of an historical period). Concrete reality gives the story the flesh without which it would be only an intellectual exercise.

We shall begin with the documentary factor. Even if *The Wrong Man* were only a faithful account of an item on the police blotter, it would be enough to justify our admiration. A man is arrested in another's place and because he is innocent has a certain distance on what he is undergoing, even if he is therefore undergoing it more intensely. Hitchcock, who enjoys dragging his characters through the mud of contempt, finds the most efficacious form for the expression of this contempt. This fascination with abjection, to which he cedes and makes us cede along with his hero, recalls Murnau's *The Last Laugh.*

Christopher Emmanuel Balestrero (Henry Fonda), a musician at the Stork Club, goes to the office of an insurance company to borrow money on his wife's policy. He is identified as the man responsible for several holdups that have taken place in the last few months, and the police pick him up in front of his door.

During the entire first part of the film we follow him through the formalities—the rites, one is tempted to say—of police and legal procedures. First there is the confrontation with witnesses: under the dull stares of the office workers or the slightly curious ones of the shopkeepers before whom he is paraded, he is reduced to anonymity, becomes something that has to be identified. Then there is the handwriting check, during which we are spared neither the actual time it takes the accused man to write nor the monotonous scratching of the pen on the paper. There is also the booking procedure—several times in the course of the film we hear him recite his name, age, and profession: "Christopher Emmanuel Balestrero, thirty-eight, musician"—the shame of being locked up in a cell and the greater one of being handcuffed, the swift routine of being charged, and, since the bail set is too high, his imprisonment, with the attendant promiscuity of the shower and the lockup.

This is a documentary without embellishments, even though the camera that shows it to us is never impassive but always descrip-

Begun in 1956, *The Wrong Man,* starring Henry Fonda and Vera Miles, used a script by Maxwell Anderson and Angus McPhail. It was based on a true story of a man falsely accused of robbery. (PHOTO COURTESY OF MUSEUM OF MODERN ART)

tive, narrative, as Hitchcock's camera always is. And this veristic detail only helps to buttress the strength of the symbol. We not only clearly discover the Idea, but—if it can be put that way—we feel it. The idea is an extremely complex one, the components of which we can successively identify as: that of the fundamental *abjectness* of a human being, who once deprived of his freedom is no more than an object among other objects; that of *misfortune,* which is simultaneously unjust and merited, like that of Job (everything seems to conspire against our musician); and that of *guilt,* as fundamental as the guilt that serves as the theme of

Kafka's *The Trial*. And as Balestrero comes to appreciate the
futility of any protest, the idea of *redemption* is grafted onto all the
others. Fonda's face and Christ-like postures in his cell recall the
iconography of the Stations of the Cross.

His brother-in-law having collected the necessary bail, the
prisoner is freed. From this point on, allegory is dominant. As we
have pointed out, everything seems to conspire against him—to an
almost unbelievable extent. His lawyer having advised him to find
witnesses, he successively learns of the death of the only two who
can furnish him with an alibi. Then his wife goes mad. Of all
Hitchcock's films this is certainly the least dependent on fiction,
but at the same time it is the most unbelievable. Because of this,
the auteur is very careful to let us know that the story is a true one.
We have here a modern application of a principle dear to
Corneille: an unusual event can be the basis for a tragedy provided
that it is also a "possible" event. And the *a fortiori* proof that it is
possible is that it happened.

Therefore, in this film the extraordinary is not, as in the
previous works, merely a motor force, a pretext for dazzling
developments. It is shown for what it is, and becomes the very
object of the study. It is then important for Hitchcock to vest it in
that privileged, perfected form which is that of the *miracle*. (*Le
vent souffle où il veut, Italian Journey,* and *Mr. Arkadin* also
showed us miracles.) Balestrero is about to be convicted when the
impromptu intervention of a juror, wearied by the lawyer's
hairsplitting, causes a mistrial. Once more he is free, but alone (his
wife has been sent to a psychiatric hospital) and more despairing
than ever. On his mother's advice he prays, and as he contem-
plates the image of the Sacred Heart, a superimposition shows us
the true criminal walking along the street and moving toward the
camera until his face dissolves into Fonda's. The man will be
caught a few minutes later: Balestrero will be cleared.

Was there really a miracle? We are given no reason to deny it;
but unlike what happens in Carl Dreyer's *Ordet,* and despite the
clear prejudices of the narrator, a certain freedom of judgment is
left us. Certainly Hitchcock has no intention of ridiculing this idea
of Providence, which we have encountered elsewhere along the

way. On the contrary, what the auteur denounces is the weak surrender to chance (significantly enough, our wrong man plays the horses in his spare time). What he excoriates more severely still are those two theological sins of presumption and despair.

The misfortune that overtakes the protagonist and his wife is extraordinary only because they consent to consider it as such. If one objectively weighs what is happening to them, there is as much good luck (the payment of the bail, the mistrial) as bad luck. Both of them are victims of their distrust in divine benevolence and the virtue of their own free will. They give way to the fascination of diabolical machination, that other Hitchcockian theme. Finally, and this is the last error of the false guilty man—who, like the rest of his earthly brothers since the Fall is only a false innocent—he believes that because one miracle has taken place, a second is his due. In this he is like that legendary shepherdess who—having been miraculously saved when she threw herself from a cliff to escape the lord of the manor—tried to repeat the exploit and ended by killing herself. But the young wife will remain mad, at least for the time being, and the nurse's words suggest that human patience will play a part in her cure . . . even though here too we are permitted to believe in the possibility of a miracle.

The conclusion is obviously ambiguous, but this is no hedge: the ambiguity is in things themselves. It is characteristic of Hitchcock to show us both sides of the coin. His work moves between two poles which, like extremes, can meet. We have called this movement "exchange": let us recognize that it here finds its most noble expression in the idea of the *interchangeable guilt* of all mankind. It retrospectively adorns with a new richness and depth the more modest or superficial aspects that it merely clothed elsewhere.

As for the form, its basic postulate is perhaps more difficult to isolate in this case, but it is no less rigorous than in the works of so-called pure virtuosity. The "matrix-figure," as is only right, will be that of the *wall*. Always skillful in taking advantage of the contingencies of actual filming, Hitchcock profited from the fact that he could not in a real decor—which was most often the same as that of the true incident—draw his camera back very far. He hugs the faces, thereby increasing our sense of suffocation. After a brief prelude on opening and shutting doors, the basic chord is struck with the scene in the office of the insurance company. From the other side of the counter the employees stare at Balestrero as they hide behind a fellow worker.

Similarly, when the musician is being driven away in a car by the police, his view is blocked by the profiles of the two detectives alongside him and by the third, of whom he can see only the forehead and eyes in the rearview mirror. This last framing device, that of a frame within a frame, will turn up again in the form of the prison-door window through which the camera penetrates and later—when he is told that the bail has been paid—withdraws, as it isolates the prisoner's two enormous eyes. Artifice? No: the royal art of a film-maker who as a worthy emulator of Murnau knows how to forcefully dehumanize a face which is at other times shown as human—all too human—thus bracketing for an instant the presence of a soul so as to make it all the more evident elsewhere; and also to humiliate what is most noble in man: the look in his eyes. This interpretation is confirmed by the broken mirror, in which we see Fonda's image deformed, and looking, as the director has noted, "like a Picasso."[1] Under the baton of a director of genius—and we need not fear to use this word—the conventional cinema is able to perform bold feats over which members of the would-be "avant garde" have stumbled in the past, are stumbling now, and will continue to stumble in the future. And it is Stravinsky of whom Hitchcock reminds us in the same scene, which is unbelievably concise. When Vera Miles strikes Fonda, we see only the start of the blow and its result, and this abruptness accentuates the strangeness of the madwoman's gesture and makes her slow return toward the bed all the more oppressive.

The most diverse styles blend very happily in this film, and their successive use in no way disturbs its perfect homogeneity. We are spared many intervals (spatial or temporal), but certain seemingly unimportant moments are evoked in exactly the time they take in real life. This is true of the previously mentioned scene of the handwriting check, or the one in which Balestrero's wife phones

[1] *Cahiers du Cinéma*, No. 62, p. 3.

the lawyer. The point of view is only seemingly subjective. Though we see things with Balestrero's own eyes (when the handcuffs are put on and there is a suggestion of his shoulder, or when he dare not look at the prisoners alongside him and sees only a row of feet on the floor of the black maria), the protagonist remains outside us, just as he is outside himself. This false subjectivity, this false exteriority, are really part of the basic atmosphere of the film.

The ambiguity of meaning corresponds to the constant ambiguity of form—which once again proves that technique is nothing in itself; what counts is the use one makes of it. The scene of the prisoner in his cell owes its tragic grandeur to the simplest of means—several shots of the walls and the ceiling—and in any other director would have seemed insipid, not to say old-fashioned—as might "on paper" have seemed that extraordinary shot with which the cell scene ends, when the camera suddenly gets dizzy and dancingly gyrates before Fonda's face.

Once the prisoner is set free, the feeling of suffocation gives way to an analogous feeling of a conspiracy of occult forces: Balestrero races through the city and countryside in search of proof, but whether we see him coming up to an empty table at a country hotel or opening a door from behind which jump, like from a jack-in-the-box, the astonished and mocking faces of two little girls caught in the middle of a game, his space is always to be limited.

In this film of night, this film of winter, this film in black and white in which Robert Burks adapts the tonality of his photography to that of the subject with no less ease than in the previous works in color, the various looks have the same privileged role they had in *I Confess*. The fixed and self-satisfied look of the witnesses; the professional looks of the police, the lawyer, the psychiatrist; the mad look of Vera Miles: the different kinds of looks by Henry Fonda (they could only be described by recounting the entire film again); and eventually the looks exchanged between the man falsely accused and the man who is really guilty, looks by means of which—as though they were transmission wires—the "exchange" takes place as the former passes his guilt to the latter. And finally, sound—the sound of objects, the sound of off-camera voices—is the focus of constant attention. The noise of the elevated train introduces a leitmotif, and Bernard Herrmann's beautiful score blends with the overall austerity of the work.

The discussion of this film, which so singularly illuminates the previous works, will serve as our peroration. In concluding, let us merely choose from among all the aspects of a multifaceted genius the one that seems the least indisputable to us. As we have said, Hitchcock is one of the greatest *inventors of form* in the entire history of cinema. Perhaps only Murnau and Eisenstein can sustain comparison with him when it comes to form. Our effort will not have been in vain if we have been able to demonstrate how an entire moral universe has been elaborated on the basis of this form and by its very rigor. In Hitchcock's work form does not embellish content, it creates it. All of Hitchcock can be summed up in this formula. *This is what we wanted to demonstrate.*

ALFRED HITCHCOCK FILMOGRAPHY (1922-1957)

Silent Films

1922—*Always Tell Your Wife* (Islington Studios).
The director having become sick during filming, Hitchcock finished the film in collaboration with the producer, Seymour Hicks.

1922—*Number Thirteen* (Wardour & F.—London). Unfinished.
Produced and directed by Alfred Hitchcock.
Director of Photography: Rosenthal.
Principal Actors: Clare Greet, Ernest Thesiger.

At the end of this same year, 1922, Famous Players-Lasky ceased production at Islington. A small crew, which included Hitchcock, was kept on by the studio. When Michael Balcon joined Victor Saville and John Freedman in founding a new independent company and shot his first film at Islington, Hitchcock was hired as assistant director.

1922—*Woman to Woman* (Balcon-Saville-Freedman).
Producer: Michael Balcon.
Director: Graham Cutts.
Assistant Director: Alfred Hitchcock.
Scenario: Graham Cutts and Alfred Hitchcock, from the play by Michael Morton.
Distributed by Wardour & F. Filmed at Islington Studios.
Principal Actors: Betty Compson, Clive Brook.

1923—*The Prude's Fall** (Balcon-Saville-Freedman).
Producer: Michael Balcon.

*Most filmographies give this as 1925—Trans.

153

Director: Graham Cutts.
Assistant Director and Decorator: Alfred Hitchcock.
Scenario: Alfred Hitchcock.
Distributed by Wardour and F. Filmed at Islington Studios.
Principal Actor: Betty Compson.

1923—*The White Shadow* (Balcon-Saville-Freedman).
Producer: Michael Balcon.
Director: Graham Cutts.
Assistant Director and Decorator: Alfred Hitchcock.
Scenario: Michael Morton.
Distributed by Wardour & F. Filmed at Islington Studios.
Principal Actors: Betty Compson, Clive Brook, Henry Victor, Daisy Campbell, Olaf Hytten, A. B. Imeson.

1924—*The Passionate Adventure* (Gainsborough—Michael Balcon's new company).
Producer: Michael Balcon.
Director: Graham Cutts.
Assistant Director and Decorator: Alfred Hitchcock.
Scenario: Alfred Hitchcock and Michael Morton.
Distributed by Gaumont. Filmed at Islington Studios.
Principal Actors: Alice Joyce, Clive Brook, Lillian Hall-Davies, Marjorie Daw, Victor McLaglen, Mary Brough, John Hamilton, J. R. Tozer.

1925—*The Blackguard* (Gainsborough).
Producer: Michael Balcon.
Director: Graham Cutts.
Assistant Director: Alfred Hitchcock.
Scenario: Alfred Hitchcock, from a novel by Raymond Paton.
Distributed by Wardour & F. Filmed at Neubabelsberg (UFA Studios).
Principal Actors: Walter Rilla, Bernard Goetzke, Jane Novak, Frank Stanmore.

Michael Balcon joined with Erich Pommer to make this film. *The Blackguard* was followed by two films shot in collaboration with Emelka at its Munich studios. Both were directed by Hitchcock.

1925—*The Pleasure Garden* (Gainsborough-Emelka).
Producer: Michael Balcon.
Director: Alfred Hitchcock.
Scenario: Eliot Stannard, from the novel by Oliver Sandys.

Director of Photography: Baron Ventigmilia.

Script Girl: Alma Reville.

Distributed by Wardour & F. Filmed at Emelka Studios-Munich.

Principal Actors: Virginia Valli, Carmelita Geraghty, Miles Mander, John Stuart, Frederick Martini, Florence Helminger.

1926—*The Mountain Eagle* (American title: *Fear O'God*) (Gainsborough Emelka).

Producer: Michael Balcon.

Director: Alfred Hitchcock.

Scenario: Eliot Stannard.

Director of Photography: Baron Ventigmilia.

Distributed by Wardour & F. Filmed at Emelka Studios-Munich and in the Austrian Tyrol.

Principal Actors: Bernard Goetzke, Nita Naldi, Malcolm Keen, John Hamilton.

1926—*The Lodger* (Gainsborough).

Producer: Michael Balcon.

Director: Alfred Hitchcock.

Scenario: Alfred Hitchcock and Eliot Stannard, from the novel by Mrs. Belloc-Lowndes.

Director of Photography: Hal Young.*

Editor: Ivor Montagu.

Distributed by Wardour & F. Filmed at Islington Studios.

Principal Actors: Ivor Novello, June, Malcolm Keen, Arthur Chesney, Marie Ault.

1927—*Downhill* (American title: *When Boys Leave Home*) (Gainsborough).

Producer: Michael Balcon.

Director: Alfred Hitchcock.

Scenario: Eliot Stannard, from a play by Ivor Novello and Constance Collier (under the pseudonym David Lestrange).

Director of Photography: Claude McDonnell.

Editor: Ivor Montagu.

Distributed by Wardour and F.

Principal Actors: Ivor Novello, Ben Webster, Robin Irvine, Sybil Rhoda, Lillian Braithwaite, Violet Farebrother, Isabel Jeans, Hannah Jones, Norman McKinnel, Jerrold Robertshaw, Annette Benson, Barbara Gott, Alfred Goddard, J. Nelson.

*Most filmographies give Baron Ventigmilia.—Trans.

ALFRED HITCHCOCK FILMOGRAPHY

1927—*Easy Virtue* (Gainsborough).
  Producer: Michael Balcon.
  Director: Alfred Hitchcock.
  Scenario: Eliot Stannard, from the play by Noel Coward.
  Director of Photography: Claude McDonnell.
  Editor: Ivor Montagu.
  Distributed by Wardour and F. Filmed at Islington Studios.
  Principal Actors: Isabel Jeans, Franklin Dyall, Eric Bransby
    Williams, Ian Hunter, Robin Irvine, Violet Farebrother, Frank
    Elliot, Darcia Deane, Dorothy Boyd, Enid Stamp-Taylor.

1927—*The Ring* (British International Pictures).
  Producer: John Maxwell.
  Director: Alfred Hitchcock.
  Scenario: Alfred Hitchcock.
  Adaptation: Alma Reville.
  Director of Photography: Jack Cox.
  Distributed by Wardour and F. Filmed at Elstree Studios.
  Principal Actors: Carl Brisson, Lillian Hall-Davies, Ian Hunter,
    Harry Terry, Gordon Harker, Billy Wells.

1928—*The Farmer's Wife* (British International Pictures).
  Producer: John Maxwell.
  Director: Alfred Hitchcock.
  Scenario: Alfred Hitchcock, from the play by Eden Philpotts.
  Director of Photography: Jack Cox.
  Distributed by Wardour and F. Filmed at Elstree Studios.
  Principal Actors: Jameson Thomas, Lillian Hall-Davies, Gordon
    Harker, Maud Gill, Louise Pounds, Olga Slade, Antonia
    Brough.

1928—*Champagne* (British International Pictures).
  Producer: John Maxwell.
  Director: Alfred Hitchcock.
  Scenario: Eliot Stannard.
  Director of Photography: Jack Cox.
  Distributed by Wardour & F. Filmed at Elstree Studios.
  Principal Actors: Betty Balfour, Gordon Harker, Jack Trevor,
    Ferdinand von Alten, Marcel Vibert, Jean Bradin.

1929—*The Manxman* (British International Pictures).
  Producer: John Maxwell.

Director: Alfred Hitchcock.
Scenario: Eliot Stannard, from the novel by Sir Hall Caine.
Director of Photography: Jack Cox.
Distributed by Wardour & F. Filmed at Elstree Studios.
Principal Actors: Carl Brisson, Malcolm Keen, Anny Ondra,
  Randle Ayrton, Clare Greet.

Sound Films

1929—*Blackmail* (British International Pictures).
  Producer: John Maxwell.
  Director: Alfred Hitchcock.
  Scenario: Alfred Hitchcock, Benn W. Levy and Charles Bennett,
    from a play by Charles Bennett.
  Director of Photography: Jack Cox.
  Music: Hubert Bath and Henry Stafford.
  Sets: Norman Arnold and Wilfred Arnold.
  Editor: Emile de Ruelle.
  Distributed by Wardour & F. Filmed at Elstree Studios.
  Principal Actors: Anny Ondra, Cyril Ritchard, John Longden,
    Sara Allgood, Charles Paton, Donald Calthrop, Hannah Jones,
    Harvey Braban, Phyllis Monkman.

1930—*Elstree Calling* (British International Pictures).
  Director: Adrian Brunel.
In this first English musical, Hitchcock directed one or two sequences,
acted in by Gordon Harker, under Brunel's supervision. (Other
directors—André Charlot, Jack Hulbert, and Paul Murray—also did parts
of this film.)

1930—*Juno and the Paycock* (British International Pictures).
  Producer: John Maxwell.
  Director: Alfred Hitchcock.
  Scenario: Alma Reville, from the play by Sean O'Casey.
  Director of Photography: Jack Cox.
  Sets: Norman Arnold.
  Distributed by Wardour & F. Filmed at Elstree Studios.
  Principal Actors: Sara Allgood, Edward Chapman, Marie O'Neill,
    Sidney Morgan, John Laurie, Dennis Wyndham, John Longden,
    Kathleen O'Regan.

1930—*Murder!* (British International Pictures).
  Producer: John Maxwell.
  Director: Alfred Hitchcock.
  Scenario: Alma Reville, from the play *Enter Sir John,* by Clemence Dane and Helen Simpson.
  Director of Photography: Jack Cox.
  Sets: John Mead.
  Editors: Emile de Ruelle, René Harrison.
  Distributed by Wardour & F. Filmed at Elstree Studios.
  Principal Actors: Herbert Marshall, Norah Baring, Phyllis Konstam, Edward Chapman, Miles Mander, Esme Chaplin, A. Brondon Thomas, Joynson Powell, Esme Percy, Donald Calthrop, Marie Wright, Hannah Jones, S. J. Warmington, R. E. Jeffrey, Clare Greet, William Fazan.

1931—*The Skin Game* (British International Pictures).
  Producer: John Maxwell.
  Director: Alfred Hitchcock.
  Scenario: Alfred Hitchcock, from the play by John Galsworthy.
  Additional Dialogue: Alma Reville.
  Director of Photography: Jack Cox.
  Editors: René Harrison, A. Gobett.
  Distributed by Wardour & F. Filmed at Elstree Studios.
  Principal Actors: Edmund Gwenn, Jill Esmond, John Longden, C. V. France, Helen Haye, Dora Gregory, Phyllis Konstam, Frank Lawton, Herbert Ross, Edward Chapman, Ronald Frankau, R. E. Jeffrey, George Bancroft.

1932—*Rich and Strange* (American title: *East of Shanghai*) (British International Pictures).
  Producer: John Maxwell.
  Director: Alfred Hitchcock.
  Scenario: Alma Reville and Val Valentine, from a theme by Dale Collins.
  Directors of Photography: Jack Cox, Charles Martin.
  Editors: René Harrison, Winifred Cooper.
  Distributed by Wardour & F. Filmed at Elstree Studios.
  Principal Actors: Henry Kendall, Joan Barry, Betty Amann, Percy Marmont, Elsie Randolph.

1932—*Number Seventeen* (British International Pictures).
  Producer: John Maxwell.

Director: Alfred Hitchcock.
Scenario: Alfred Hitchcock, from the play by Jefferson Farjeon.
Director of Photography: Jack Cox.
Distributed by Wardour & F. Filmed at Elstree Studios.
Principal Actors: Léon M. Lion, Anne Grey, John Stuart, Donald Calthrop, Barry Jones, Garry Marsh.

1932—*Lord Camber's Ladies* (British International Pictures).
Producer: Alfred Hitchcock.
Director: Benn W. Levy.
Scenario: Benn W. Levy, from the play *The Case of Lady Camber*, by Horace Annesley Vachell.
Distributed by Wardour & F. Filmed at Elstree Studios.
Principal Actors: Gertrude Lawrence, Sir Gerald du Maurier, Benita Hume, Nigel Bruce.

1933—*Waltzes from Vienna* (American title: *Strauss' Great Waltz*). (Gaumont British).
Producer: Tom Arnold.
Director: Alfred Hitchcock.
Scenario: Alma Reville and Guy Bolton.
Music: Johann Strauss, father and son.
Sets: Alfred Junge, Peter Proud.
Distributed by G.F.D. Filmed at Lime Grove Studios.
Principal Actors: Jessie Matthews, Edmond Knight, Frank Vosper, Edmund Gwenn, Fay Compton, Robert Hale, Hindle Edgar, Marcus Barron, Charles Heslop, Sybil Grove, Bill Shine, B. M. Lewis, Cyril Smith, Betty Huntley Wright, Bertram Dench.

1934—*The Man Who Knew Too Much* (Gaumont British).
Producers: Michael Balcon and Ivor Montagu.
Director: Alfred Hitchcock.
Scenario: A. R. Rawlinson and Edwin Greenwood, from an original subject by D. B. Wyndham Lewis and Charles Bennett.
Additional Dialogue: Emlyn Williams.
Director of Photography: Curt Courant.
Sets: Alfred Junge, Peter Proud.
Music: Arthur Benjamin and Louis Levy.
Editor: H. St. C. Stewart.
Distributed by G.F.D. Filmed at Lime Grove Studios.
Principal Actors: Leslie Banks, Peter Lorre, Edna Best, Nova

Pilbeam, Hugh Wakefield, Pierre Fresnay, Frank Vosper, George Curzon, Cicely Oates, D. A. Clarke Smith.

1935—*The Thirty-Nine Steps* (Gaumont British).
Producers: Michael Balcon and Ivor Montagu.
Director: Alfred Hitchcock.
Scenario: Charles Bennett, from the novel by John Buchan.
Adaptation: Alma Reville.
Additional Dialogue: Ian Hay.
Director of Photography: Bernard Knowles.
Sets: Otto Werndorff and Albert Jullion.
Costumes: J. Strassner.
Music: Louis Levy.
Editor: Derek Twist.
Distributed by G.F.D. Filmed at Lime Grove Studios.
Principal Actors: Robert Donat, Madeleine Carroll, Lucie Mannheim, Godfrey Tearle, John Laurie, Peggy Ashcroft, Helen Haye, Wylie Watson, Peggy Simpson, Gus McNaughton, Jerry Verno.

1936—*The Secret Agent* (Gaumont British).
Producers: Michael Balcon and Ivor Montagu.
Director: Alfred Hitchcock.
Scenario: Charles Bennett, from a play by Campbell Dixon adapted from the novel *Ashenden* by Somerset Maugham.
Adaptation: Alma Reville.
Additional Dialogue: Ian Hay and Jesse Lasky, Jr.
Director of Photography: Bernard Knowles.
Sets: Otto Werndorff, Albert Jullion.
Costumes: J. Strassner.
Music: Louis Levy.
Editor: Charles Frend.
Distributed by G.F.D. Filmed at Lime Grove Studios.
Principal Actors: Madeleine Carroll, John Gielgud, Peter Lorre, Robert Young, Percy Marmont, Florence Kahn, Lilli Palmer, Charles Carson.

1936—*Sabotage* (American title: *A Woman Alone*) (Gaumont British).
Producers: Michael Balcon and Ivor Montagu.
Director: Alfred Hitchcock.
Scenario: Charles Bennett, from the novel *The Secret Agent,* by Joseph Conrad.

Adaptation: Alma Reville.
Additional Dialogue: Ian Hay, E. V. H. Emmett, Helen Simpson.
Director of Photography: Bernard Knowles.
Sets: Otto Werndorff, Albert Jullion.
Costumes: J. Strassner.
Music: Louis Levy.
Editing: Charles Frend.
Distributed by G.F.D. Filmed at Lime Grove Studios.
Principal Actors: Sylvia Sidney, Oscar Homolka, Desmond Tester, John Loder, Joyce Barbour, Matthew Boulton, S. J. Warmington, William Dewhurst, Peter Bull, Torin Thatcher, Austin Trevor, Clare Greet, Sam Wilkinson, Sara Allgood, Martita Hunt, Pamela Bevan.

1937—*Young and Innocent* (American title: *The Girl Was Young*) (Gainsborough–Gaumont British).
Producer: Edward Black.
Director: Alfred Hitchcock.
Scenario: Charles Bennett, from the novel *A Shilling for Candles,* by Josephine Tey.
Adaptation: Alma Reville.
Director of Photography: Bernard Knowles.
Sets: Alfred Junge.
Music: Louis Levy.
Distributed by G.F.D. Filmed at Lime Grove and Pinewood Studios.
Principal Actors: Derrick de Marney, Nova Pilbeam, Percy Marmont, Edward Rigby, Mary Clare, John Longden, George Curzon, Basil Radford, Pamela Carme, George Merritt, J. H. Roberts, Jerry Verno, H. F. Maltby, John Miller, Torin Thatcher, Peggy Simpson, Anna Konstam.

1938—*The Lady Vanishes* (Gainsborough).
Producer: Edward Black.
Director: Alfred Hitchcock
Scenario: Sidney Gilliat and Frank Launder, from the novel *The Wheel Spins,* by Ethel Lina White.
Adaptation: Alma Reville.
Director of Photography: Jack Cox.
Sets: Alec Vetchinsky, Maurice Cater, Albert Jullion.
Music: Louis Levy.

Editor: R. E. Dearing.

Distributed by MGM. Filmed at Lime Grove Studios.

Principal Actors: Margaret Lockwood, Michael Redgrave, Paul Lukas, Dame May Whitty, Googie Withers, Cecil Parker, Linden Travers, Mary Clare, Naunton Wayne, Basil Radford, Emile Boreo, Sally Stewart, Philippe Leaver, Zelma Vas Dias, Catherine Lacey, Josephine Wilson, Charles Oliver, Kathleen Tremaine.

1939—*Jamaica Inn* (Mayflower Productions).

Producers: Erich Pommer and Charles Laughton.

Director: Alfred Hitchcock.

Scenario: Sidney Gilliat and Joan Harrison, from the novel by Daphne du Maurier.

Additional Dialogue: J. B. Priestley.

Directors of Photography: Harry Stradling, Bernard Knowles.

Sets: Tom Morahan.

Music: Eric Fenby.

Editor: Robert Hamer.

Distributed by Associated British. Filmed at Elstree Studios.

Principal Actors: Maureen O'Hara, Charles Laughton, Robert Newton, Emlyn Williams, Leslie Banks, Horace Hodges, Hay Petrie, Frederick Piper, Marie Ney, Wylie Watson, Morland Graham, Edwin Greenwood, Mervyn Johns, Stephen Haggard, Herbert Lomas, Clare Greet, William Devlin, Basil Radford, Jeanne de Casalis, George Curzon, Mabel Terry Lewis, A. Bromley Davenport.

American Films

1940—*Rebecca* (David O. Selznick).

Producer: David O. Selznick.

Director: Alfred Hitchcock.

Scenario: Robert E. Sherwood and Joan Harrison, from the novel by Daphne du Maurier.

Adaptation: Philip MacDonald and Michael Hogan.

Director of Photography: George Barnes.

Music: Franz Waxman.

Sets: Herbert Bristol*

*Other filmographies give this as Lyle Wheeler.—Trans.

Editor: Hal Kern.

Distributed by United Artists. Filmed at Selznick International Studios.

Principal Actors: Laurence Olivier, Joan Fontaine, George Sanders, Judith Anderson, Nigel Bruce, C. Aubrey Smith, Reginald Denny, Gladys Cooper, Philip Winter, Edward Fielding, Florence Bates, Melville Cooper, Leo G. Carroll, Forrester Harvey, Lumsden Hare, Leonard Carey.

1940—*Foreign Correspondent* (Walter Wanger, United Artists).

Producer: Walter Wanger.

Director: Alfred Hitchcock.

Scenario: Charles Bennett and Joan Harrison.

Dialogue: James Hilton and Robert Benchley.

Director of Photography: Rudolph Mate.

Sets: William Cameron Menzies, Alexander Golitzen.

Music: Alfred Newman.

Editors: Otto Lovering, Dorothy Spencer.

Distributed by United Artists. Filmed at United Artists Studios.

Principal Actors: Joel McCrea, Laraine Day, Herbert Marshall, George Sanders, Albert Basserman, Robert Benchley, Edmund Gwenn, Harry Davenport, Eduardo Cianelli, Martin Kosleck, Eddie Conrad, Cranford Kent, Gertrude W. Hoffman, Jane Novak, Joan Brodel-Leslie, Louis Borell, Elly Malyon, E. E. Clive.

1941—*Mr. and Mrs. Smith* (RKO).

Producer: Harry Edington.

Director: Alfred Hitchcock.

Scenario: Norman Krasna.

Director of Photography: Harry Stradling.

Music: Roy Webb.

Editor: William Hamilton.

Distributed by RKO Radio. Filmed at RKO Radio Studios.

Principal Actors: Carole Lombard, Robert Montgomery, Gene Raymond, Jack Carson, Philip Merivale, Lucile Watson, William Tracy, Charles Halton, Esther Dale, Emma Dunn, Betty Compson, Patricia Farr, William Edmunds, Adele Pearce.

1941—*Suspicion* (RKO).

Director: Alfred Hitchcock.

Scenario: Samson Raphaelson, Joan Harrison, and Alma Reville, from the novel *Before the Fact,* by Francis Iles (Anthony Berkeley).

Director of Photography: Harry Stradling.

Sets: Van Nest Polglase, Darrell Silvera.*

Costumes: Edward Stevenson.

Music: Franz Waxman.

Editor: William Hamilton.

Distributed by RKO Radio. Filmed at RKO Radio Studios.

Principal Actors: Cary Grant, Joan Fontaine, Sir Cedric Hardwicke, Nigel Bruce, Dame May Whitty, Isabel Jeans, Heather Angel, Auriol Lee, Reginald Sheffield, Leo G. Carroll.

1942—*Saboteur* (Universal).

Producers: Frank Lloyd and Jack Skirball.

Director: Alfred Hitchcock.

Scenario: Peter Viertel, Joan Harrison, and Dorothy Parker, from an original subject by Alfred Hitchcock.

Director of Photography: Joseph Valentine.

Sets: Jack Otterson.

Music: Charles Previn.

Distributed by Universal. Filmed at Universal Studios.

Principal Actors: Robert Cummings, Priscilla Lane, Otto Kruger, Alan Baxter, Clem Bevans, Norman Lloyd, Alma Kruger, Vaughan Glazer, Dorothy Peterson, Ian Wolfe, Frances Carson, Murray Alper, Kathryn Adams, Pedro de Cordoba, Billy Curtis, Anita Le Deaux, Anita Bolster, Jeanne and Lynn Romer.

1943—*Shadow of a Doubt* (Universal).

Producer: Jack H. Skirball.

Director: Alfred Hitchcock.

Scenario: Thornton Wilder, Alma Reville, and Sally Benson, from a subject by Gordon McDonnell.

Director of Photography: Joseph Valentine.

Sets: John B. Goodman, R. A. Gausman.

Music: Dimitri Tiomkin, Charles Previn.

Costumes: Adrian and Vera West.

Editor: Milton Carruth.

Distributed by Universal. Filmed at Universal Studios.

Principal Actors: Joseph Cotten, Teresa Wright, MacDonald Carey, Patricia Collinge, Henry Travers, Hume Cronyn, Wal-

---

*Other filmographies give Carroll Clark.

lace Ford, Charlie Bates, Edna May Wonacott, Irving Bacon, Clarence Muse, Janet Shaw, Estelle Jewell.

1943—*Lifeboat* (Twentieth Century–Fox).
Producer: Kenneth MacGowan.
Director: Alfred Hitchcock.
Scenario: Jo Swerling, from an original subject by John Steinbeck.
Director of Photography: Glen MacWilliams.
Sets: James Basevi, Maurice Ransford.
Music: Hugo Friedhofer.
Distributed by Twentieth Century–Fox. Filmed at Twentieth Century–Fox Studios.
Principal Actors: Tallulah Bankhead, William Bendix, Walter Slezak, Mary Anderson, John Hodiak, Henry Hull, Heather Angel, Hume Cronyn, Canada Lee.

1944—*Aventure Malgache* (M.O.I.).
Short subject produced in French by the British Ministry of Information.
Director: Alfred Hitchcock.
Director of Photography: Gunther Krampf.
Sets: Charles Gilbert.
Filmed at Associated British Studios.
Principal Actors: The Molière Players (French actors who had fled to England).

1944—*Bon Voyage* (M.O.I.).
Short subject produced in French by the British Ministry of Information.
Director: Alfred Hitchcock.
Scenario: J. O. C. Orton, Angus McPhail, from an original subject by Arthur Calder-Marshall.
Director of Photography: Gunther Krampf.
Sets: Charles Gilbert.
Filmed at Associated British Studios.
Principal Actors: John Blythe and The Molière Players.

1945—*Spellbound* (Selznick International).
Producer: David O. Selznick.
Director: Alfred Hitchcock.
Scenario: Ben Hecht, from the novel *The House of Dr. Edwardes,* by Francis Beeding (Hilary St. George Saunders and John Palmer).

Adaptation: Angus McPhail.
Director of Photography: George Barnes.
Sets: James Basevi, John Ewing.
Music: Miklos Rozsa.
Editor: William Ziegler.
Distributed by United Artists. Filmed at Selznick International Studios.
Principal Actors: Ingrid Bergman, Gregory Peck, Rhonda Fleming, Leo G. Carroll, Michael Chekhov, Jean Acker, Donald Curtis, John Emery, Norman Lloyd, Steven Geray, Paul Harvey, Erskine Sanford, Victor Kilian, Wallace Ford, Bill Goodwin, Dave Willock, Janet Scott, Regis Toomey, Addison Richards, Art Baker, George Meader.

1946—*Notorious* (RKO Radio).
Producer: Alfred Hitchcock.
Director: Alfred Hitchcock.
Scenario: Ben Hecht, from a subject by Alfred Hitchcock.
Director of Photography: Ted Tetzlaff.
Sets: Albert S. D'Agostino, Carroll Clark, Darrell Silvera.
Costumes: Edith Head.
Music: Roy Webb, F. Bakaleinikoff.
Editor: Theron Warth.
Distributed by RKO Radio. Filmed at RKO Radio Studios.
Principal Actors: Ingrid Bergman, Cary Grant, Claude Rains, Louis Calhern, Mme. Konstantin, Reinhold Schunzel, Moroni Olsen, Ivan Triesault, Alexis Minotis, Eberhardt Krumschmidt, Fay Baker, Peter von Zerneck, Lenore Ulric, Ramon Nomar, Sir Charles Mendl, Ricardo Costa.

1947—*The Paradine Case* (Selznick International).
Producer: David O. Selznick.
Director: Alfred Hitchcock.
Scenario: David O. Selznick, from the novel by Robert Hichens.
Adaptation: Alma Reville.
Director of Photography: Lee Garmes.
Sets: J. MacMillan Johnson, Thomas Morahan.
Costumes: Travis Banton.
Music: Franz Waxman.
Editors: Hal C. Kern and John Faure.
Distributed by United Artists. Filmed at Selznick International Studios.

Principal Actors: Gregory Peck, Ann Todd, Charles Laughton, Charles Coburn, Ethel Barrymore, Louis Jourdan, Alida Valli, Joan Tetzel, Leo G. Carroll, John Goldsworthy, Lester Matthew, Pat Aherne, Colin Hunter, Isobel Elsom.

1948—*Rope* (Transatlantic Pictures). Technicolor.
Producers: Sidney Bernstein and Alfred Hitchcock.
Director: Alfred Hitchcock.
Scenario: Arthur Laurents, from the play by Patrick Hamilton.
Adaptation: Hume Cronyn.
Directors of Photography: Joseph Valentine, William V. Skall.
Sets: Perry Ferguson.
Costumes: Adrian.
Music: Leo F. Forbstein, based on Francis Poulenc's *Perpetual Movement No. 1.*
Editor: William Ziegler.
Distributed by Warner Bros. Filmed at Warner Bros. Studios.
Principal Actors: James Stewart, John Dall, Farley Granger, Joan Chandler, Sir Cedric Hardwicke, Constance Collier, Edith Evanson, Douglas Dick, Dick Hogan.

1949—*Under Capricorn* (Transatlantic Pictures). Technicolor.
Producers: Sidney Bernstein and Alfred Hitchcock.
Director: Alfred Hitchcock.
Scenario: James Bridie, from the novel by Helen Simpson.
Adaptation: Hume Cronyn.
Director of Photography: Jack Cardiff.
Sets: Thomas Morahan.
Costumes: Roger Furse.
Music: Richard Addinsell, Louis Levy.
Editor: A. S. Bates.
Distributed by Warner Bros. Filmed at MGM British Studios, Elstree.
Principal Actors: Ingrid Bergman, Joseph Cotten, Michael Wilding, Margaret Leighton, Jack Watling, Cecil Parker, Denis O'Dea, Olive Sloan, Maureen Delaney, Julia Lang, Betty McDermot, Bill Shine, John Ruddock, Roderick Lovell, Ronald Adam, G. H. Mulcaster, Victor Lucas, Francis de Wolff.

1950—*Stage Fright* (Warner Bros.).
Producers: Alfred Hitchcock and Fred Ahern.
Scenario: Whitfield Cook, from "Man Running" and "Outrun the Constable," stories by Selwyn Jepson.

Adaptation: Alma Reville.
Additional Dialogue: James Bridie.
Director of Photography: Wilkie Cooper.
Sets: Terence Verity.
Music: Leighton Lucas, Louis Levy.
Editor: Edward Jarvis.
Distributed by Warner Bros. Filmed at Elstree Studios.
Principal Actors: Marlene Dietrich, Jane Wyman, Michael Wild-
ing, Richard Todd, Alastair Sim, Dame Sybil Thorndike, Kay
Walsh, Miles Malleson, Hector MacGregor, Joyce Grenfell,
André Morell, Patricia Hitchcock.

1951—*Strangers on a Train* (Warner Bros.).
Producer: Alfred Hitchcock.
Director: Alfred Hitchcock.
Scenario: Raymond Chandler, Czenzi Ormonde, from the novel by
Patricia Highsmith.
Adaptation: Whitfield Cook.
Director of Photography: Robert Burks.
Sets: Ted Haworth, George James Hopkins.
Costumes: Leah Rhodes.
Music: Dimitri Tiomkin, Ray Heindorf.
Editor: William H. Ziegler.
Distributed by Warner Bros. Filmed at Warner Bros. Studios.
Principal Actors: Farley Granger, Robert Walker, Ruth Roman,
Leo G. Carroll, Patricia Hitchcock, Laura Elliot, Marion Lorne,
Jonathan Hale, Howard St. John, John Brown, Norma Varden,
Robert Gist, John Doucette.

1952—*I Confess* (Warner Bros.).
Producer: Alfred Hitchcock.
Director: Alfred Hitchcock.
Scenario: George Tabori, William Archibald, from the play *Nos
deux consciences,* by Paul Anthelme.
Director of Photography: Robert Burks.
Decorators: Edward S. Haworth, George James Hopkins.
Costumes: Orry Kelly.
Music: Dimitri Tiomkin, Ray Heindorf.
Editor: Rudi Fehr.
Technical Consultant: Father Paul LaCouline.
Distributed by Warner Bros. Filmed in Quebec and in Warner
Bros. Studios.

Principal Actors: Montgomery Clift, Anne Baxter, Karl Malden, Brian Aherne, O. E. Hasse, Roger Dann, Dolly Haas, Charles André, Judson Pratt, Ovila Legare, Gilles Pelletier.

1954—*Dial M for Murder* (Warner Bros.). Naturalvision and 3-D. Warnercolor.
Producer: Alfred Hitchcock.
Director: Alfred Hitchcock.
Scenario: Frederick Knott, from his play.
Director of Photography: Robert Burks.
Sets: Edward Carrère, George James Hopkins.
Costumes: Moss Mabry.
Music: Dimitri Tiomkin.
Editor: Rudi Fehr.
Distributed by Warner Bros. Filmed at Warner Bros. Studios.
Principal Actors: Ray Milland, Grace Kelly, Robert Cummings, John Williams, Anthony Dawson, Leo Britt, Patrick Allen, George Leigh, George Alderson, Robin Hughes.

1954—*Rear Window* (Paramount). Technicolor.
Producer: Alfred Hitchcock.
Director: Alfred Hitchcock.
Scenario: John Michael Hayes, from the novel by Cornell Woolrich.
Director of Photography: Robert Burks.
Sets: Sam Comer and Ray Mayer.
Music: Lynn Murray.
Costumes: Edith Head.
Principal Actors: James Stewart, Grace Kelly, Wendell Corey, Thelma Ritter, Raymond Burr, Judith Evelyn, Ross Bagdasarian, Georgine Darcy, Jesslyn Fax, Irene Winston.

1955—*To Catch a Thief* (Paramount). VistaVision. Technicolor.
Producer: Alfred Hitchcock.
Director: Alfred Hitchcock.
Scenario: John Michael Hayes, from a novel by David Dodge.
Director of Photography: Robert Burks.
Sets: Sam Comer and Arthur Crams.
Music: Lynn Murray.
Costumes: Edith Head.
Principal Actors: Cary Grant, Grace Kelly, Brigitte Auber, Charles Vanel, Jessie Royce Landis, John Williams, Roland

Lesaffre, Georgette Anys, Jean Martinelli, Jean Hebey, Gerard Buhr, René Blancard.

1956—*The Trouble with Harry* (Paramount). VistaVision. Technicolor.
Producer: Alfred Hitchcock.
Director: Alfred Hitchcock.
Scenario: John Michael Hayes, from the novel by John Trevor Story.
Director of Photography: Robert Burks.
Sets: Sam Comer, Emile Kuri.
Music: Bernard Herrmann.
Editor: Alma Macrorie.
Distributed by Paramount.
Principal Actors: Edmund Gwenn, John Forsythe, Shirley MacLaine, Mildred Natwick, Mildred Dunnock, Royal Dano, Parker Fennelly, Barry Macollum, Dwight Marfield.

1956—*The Man Who Knew Too Much* (Paramount). VistaVision. Technicolor.
Producer: Alfred Hitchcock.
Director: Alfred Hitchcock.
Scenario: John Michael Hayes and Angus McPhail, from a story by Charles Bennett and D. B. Wyndham-Lewis.
Director of Photography: Robert Burks.
Sets: Sam Comer and Arthur Krams.
Costumes: Edith Head.
Music: Bernard Herrmann.
Editor: George Tomasini.
Distributed by Paramount.
Principal Actors: James Stewart, Doris Day, Daniel Gélin, Brenda de Banzie, Bernard Miles, Ralph Truman, Mogens Wieth, Christopher Olsen.

1957—*The Wrong Man* (Warner Bros.).
Producer: Alfred Hitchcock.
Director: Alfred Hitchcock.
Scenario: Maxwell Anderson and Angus McPhail, from "The True Story of Christopher Emmanuel Balestrero," by Maxwell Anderson.
Director of Photography: Robert Burks.
Sets: William L. Kuehl.
Music: Bernard Herrmann.

Editor: George Tomasini.

Principal Actors: Henry Fonda, Vera Miles, Anthony Quayle, Harold J. Stone, Charles Cooper, John Heldabrand, Esther Minciotti, Doreen Lang, Laurinda Barrett, Richard Robbins, Norma Connolly.

INDEX

173